Resilient Faith

Navigating Life's Challenges using Islamic Wisdom to Achieve Strength and Inner Peace

SARAH GULFRAZ

Copyright © 2024 Sarah Gulfraz

Sarah Gulfraz has asserted her right to be identified as the author of this Work in accordance with the Copyright, Designs and Patents Act 1988.

All rights reserved.

No portion of this book may be reproduced in any form, stored in a retrieval system, stored in a database, or published/transmitted in any form or by any means, electronic, mechanical, photocopying, recording or otherwise, without prior written permission of the publisher.

Dedication

~ Bismillah ~

May Allah (swt) accept our efforts and grant us success in this life and the next. Ameen.

In dedication to my loving family and all their support.

Contents

Chapter One

Introduction

Life is a journey filled with triumphs and trials, each presenting its own set of challenges. No doubt, facing difficulties is an inevitable part of our existence. As Muslims, we believe our life's challenges and hardships serve as a means of putting our faith and allegiance to Allah (SWT) to the test so that we can be rewarded in this world and the hereafter.

These times are opportunities to deepen our faith and hone our moral fibre rather than penalties. We gain inner strength and blessings when we patiently face these challenges and have faith in Allah's (SWT) great plan.

Islam gives us an outlook that sees this world as a temporary home, where Allah (SWT) tests us people solely to strengthen our faith when it falters, to atone for our transgressions, and to bring out the best in each of us. In times of hardship, we as Muslims must draw on spiritual insights and practical advice, which provide a roadmap for navigating life's hurdles with unwavering faith and inner peace.

During his life, the Prophet Muhammad (PBUH) encountered many difficulties. He was made fun of, harassed, and even had to leave his native Makkah. Yet, he bore these trials with unshakable patience, setting a strong example for Muslims.

With its foundation in the timeless teachings of Islam, this book intended to assist you in meeting life's obstacles head-on, with courage and composure.

These emotions can frequently feel like navigating a tumultuous sea, especially when it comes to mental health. The wisdom of Islamic teachings acts as a light of hope, guiding us toward the shores of inner calm amid these turbulent emotional waters. This book explores how Islamic teachings act as a compass for changing our feelings, leading us from the abyss of rage to the calm of peace.

The lessons in this book serve as beacons of light, providing a clear road map for navigating the complexity of rage and how it affects mental health. By incorporating these lessons into our daily lives, we can become more resilient, foster inner serenity and enhance our mental health and well-being.

This thorough book also discusses Islamic methods for overcoming adversity while maintaining religion and spiritual development. To assist readers in conquering hardship and succeeding in both the material and spiritual spheres of life, each chapter provides insightful analysis and doable and concrete actions based on the teachings of the Quran and the traditions of the Prophets.

Let's dive in!

Chapter Two

Understanding Life's Challenges

Recognising the Nature of Life's Trials and Tribulations

There is no denying that this earthly life is full of trials and tribulations. Individual differences exist in what defines a trial or tribulation. Still, all people are tested on some level—whether in terms of ease or difficulty, money, relationships, health, or other areas.

Those who came before us were likewise put to the test, and neither the strong nor the devout were spared. Numerous individuals highly esteemed by Allah (SWT) underwent significant trials. These trials remind each of us of how we overcame adversity and the rewards of persistence.

Within the Islamic faith, hardships are frequently perceived as purposeful divine interventions meant to evaluate an individual's faith, fortitude, and loyalty. These assessments are meant to show a believer's genuine nature and level of confidence in Allah (SWT), not to punish them. Like prophets and righteous people in religious stories, Muslims show their dedication to and devotion to Allah (SWT) by bearing these tribulations with patience and unflinching faith.

From an Islamic perspective, these trials and tribulations are tests from Allah (SWT) that offer opportunities for spiritual development and build a deeper connection with the Divine. Islam also provides guidance that these trials and tribulations are accompanied by effective ways to endure them with patience, maintain gratitude, and seek support from the community. Quran and Hadith (sayings of the Prophet Muhammad PBUH) are the basic sources that provide a comprehensive framework for coping with life's trials and tribulations.

> *Allah (SWT) says: "And We will surely test you with something of fear and hunger and a loss of wealth and lives and fruits, but give good tidings to the patient, who, when disaster strikes them, say, 'Indeed we belong to Allah (SWT), and indeed to Him we will return.' Those are the ones upon who are blessings from their Lord and mercy. And it is those who are the rightly guided."*
> *(Quran 2:155-157)*

This clearly shows that the Quran supports the fact that trials and tribulations are from Allah (SWT), and believers' patience and proper response lead to divine blessings and guidance.

> *The Holy Prophet (PBUH) said that: "A believer may be tested according to the measure of his religion. If his religion is strong, his test is severe; and if his religion is weak, his test is light. Trials will continue to befall the believer until he walks upon the earth without any sin."*
> *(Sahih Muslim)*

Islam promotes the understanding that trials are not random or meaningless. They are signs of Allah's (SWT) positive intention towards the believers, intended for their benefit and growth. It's a divine plan to guide believers in their spiritual journey. Let's look at this in detail!

Exploring common challenges faced in personal, professional, and spiritual spheres

Life gives us a different set of obstacles every day. Sometimes, we feel like giving up, and other times, we feel like we can conquer the world and win. Every day is an adventure in life, a never-ending rollercoaster. No matter how old we are or how we live, there will always be challenges in our lives. They might make us feel overwhelmed and like giving up. They can take many different shapes and ultimately cover our spiritual, professional, and personal spheres of life.

But it's important to recognise that challenges are more than just difficult. They serve as growth-promoting catalysts, inspiring us to go above and beyond our comfort zones, reveal our inner capabilities, and build resilience. Muslims handle these difficulties using the directions given by the Quran and Sunnah, which provide a road map for successfully navigating them. Let's explore these problems' capacity to transform, how they can mould our personalities and their enormous effects on our lives as a whole.

Personal Sphere

Taking on personal challenges is about becoming a better version of yourself; it's not only about reaching predetermined goals. These tasks are intended to gently but forcefully force you to step outside your everyday routine and comfort zone to explore new areas of possibility. Changing your behaviour, picking up new skills, or adopting healthier habits—every step you take will lead to a more satisfying existence.

While contemplating embracing personal challenges, consider them investments in your most valuable resource: yourself. Your potential for personal development and fulfilment is boundless if you possess these qualities along with the appropriate resources and perseverance. Let's examine these major kinds of challenges in detail!

Maintaining Personal Discipline

The most common challenge we face in our daily lives is maintaining personal discipline amidst our daily responsibilities. To achieve a desired lifestyle and identity, personal discipline involves controlling one's behaviour, accepting responsibility for one's own actions, and establishing new routines and norms. When challenged with distractions, hardships, or temptations, personal discipline entails the persistent application of self-control, confidence, and adherence to predefined norms or principles.

Islam emphasises the importance of discipline as a fundamental component of spiritual and human growth. One of the main themes of the Quran is self-discipline. Islam places great importance on the capacity to restrain one's passions, make moral choices, and maintain composure in the face of difficulty.

Islam places a high value on discipline, which helps to create morally upright individuals and a just and harmonious community. This emphasis is evident in many facets of worship, conduct, and interpersonal relationships.

For example, as Muslims, we are called to maintain a disciplined approach to the regular practice of the five daily prayers (Salah), fasting (Sawm) during the month of Ramadan, giving charity (Zakat), and fulfilling all other religious obligations.

Self-discipline is simply a balance among all the religious obligations with other personal duties in life. Achieving this balance can be demanding, but Islam provides a comprehensive guideline for Muslims to attain self-discipline through Taqwa (God-consciousness) and the remembrance of Allah (SWT). Through these practices, we can maintain focus, align our intentions, and better manage our lifestyle accordingly. A life of self-discipline brings numerous benefits, including inner peace and contentment, while freeing up time and resources to be used more wisely.

Surah Al-Baqarah emphasises the significance of self-discipline in avoiding temptation and requesting Allah's (SWT) assistance: "Allah (SWT) does not burden a soul beyond that it can bear...Our Lord, do not impose blame upon us if we forget or make a mistake. Our Lord, and lay not upon us a burden like that which you laid upon those before us. Our Lord, and burden us not with that which we have no ability to bear." (Quran 2:286)

This verse reminds believers that self-discipline entails acknowledging one's limitations and depending on Allah's (SWT) direction to overcome difficult situations.

As a Muslim, you can practise self-discipline by worshipping Allah (SWT), remaining in His presence and surrendering to Him, reading the Quran, reading helpful religious texts, attending educational events, and surrounding yourself with good people.

Moreover, self-discipline is also linked with admitting your mistakes. Acknowledging your shortcomings is the first step towards developing self-discipline, and it motivates you to continually improve.

This acknowledgement is one of the things that drive us to discipline ourselves consistently. You shouldn't let this admission discourage you from self-discipline. As Allah (SWT) said, when a person makes an effort to grow and evolve, it indicates Allah's (SWT) concern.

"Verily, Allah (SWT) will not change the condition of a people as long as they do not change their state themselves." (Quran 13:11)

Thus, developing self-discipline is one of the most significant personal challenges that one must learn to tackle in life. Lack of self-discipline can lead to a number of issues and things stacking up and overwhelming you, and it can also divert you from your moral and religious obligations. Thus, it's crucial to cultivate this talent.

Managing Emotional Well-being

At some point in our lives, we may experience emotional crises that can be difficult to handle. These crises can be brought on by a number of things, including marital troubles, health problems, financial difficulties, or the unexpected death of a loved one.

We frequently endure emotional, mental, physical and behavioural distress during these periods. Emotional challenges are common in modern life. Islam's teachings, derived from the Quran and Sunnah, offer us support, stability, resources, and help as we get through these trying times.

According to the Quran, there will undoubtedly be hardships in our worldly lives. Each person will encounter unique obstacles, such as psychological difficulties. The verse below highlights a few of these feelings, including fear, anxiety, worries, and concern.

> *"We will surely test you with something of fear and hunger and a loss of wealth and lives and fruits, but give good tidings to the patient." (Quran 2: 155)*

All people experience sadness, anxiety, and worry to varying degrees as normal emotions. These feelings were also experienced by Allah's (SWT) unique creatures, the prophets. So, we must recognise and accept our emotions and feelings.

In addition, the Quran gives Muslims hope by emphasising that ease always follows hardship.

"For indeed, with hardship [will be] ease. Indeed, with hardship [will be] ease." (Quran: 94; 5-6)

This repetition emphasises how relief is always guaranteed after adversity. We learn from the Quran to maintain optimism in times of crisis.

As Muslims, we ought to believe Allah (SWT) is the Almighty Who Grants Requests and Is Receptive to Them. He is available for us to call upon at any time—in times of need, in times of joy, and moments of thankfulness. Thus, offer up prayers. One very effective instrument Allah (SWT) has provided believers is prayer.

Allah (SWT) assures His devoted followers that He will respond to our calls. Trusting Allah's (SWT) plans and relying on his help is the best way to attain emotional stability.

In addition to all of the above, sustaining spirituality preserves mental health. A vital component of mental wellness is spirituality. It's important to realise that being spiritual involves more than just doing your religious obligations. It is possible to practise all religions without really becoming spiritual. A true spiritual practice is making a constant effort to be closer to Allah (SWT) using the ability we have. Maintaining a relationship with the Creator can restore lost peace of mind and enhance our overall well-being.

The Prophet (PBUH) said, "Whoever is afflicted with sadness or anxiety, let him pray with these words: 'O Allah (SWT), I am Your servant, son of Your male servant and son of Your female servant. My forehead is in Your hand. Your judgment upon me is assured, and Your decree upon me is just. I ask You by every name that You have, which You have revealed in Your Book, taught to

*any of Your creation, or You have kept to Yourself in the
knowledge of the unseen that is with You, to make the
Quran the spring of my heart, the light of my chest, the
banisher of my sadness, and the reliever of my distress.'"
(Sahih Ahmad)*

Building and Maintaining Relationships

Managing relationships can be challenging for several reasons, particularly because they force us to adapt and change. Each of us brings our own viewpoints, convictions, and behaviours into relationships. When two people interact, conflicts, arguments, and the necessity for compromise often arise. As a result, building and maintaining these social interactions can be demanding.

In Islam, Muslims are always encouraged to maintain good relationships with others. In personal relationships, Islam ordered Adab (manners) and Husn al-Khulq (good conduct).

*The Prophet Muhammad (PBUH) said, "The best of you
are those who are best in character and the most patient
in dealing with people." (Musnad Ahmad)*

This hadith also teaches us the value of patience and good moral character when interacting with people. For the sake of Allah (SWT), we are urged to establish relationships based on love, respect, and compassion guided by our faith.

*Prophet Muhammad (PBUH) said, "None of you [truly]
believes until he loves for his brother that which he loves
for himself." (Bukhari and Muslim)*

This hadith serves as a reminder of our duty to treat our loved ones, neighbours, and fellow citizens with respect and compassion, upholding their rights and offering assistance when required. In the same way, the Prophet (PBUH) demonstrated this to his companions by urging them to look out for one another.

Our lives are significantly impacted by the interactions we have with our loved ones. These relationships provide emotional support, company, and a feeling of belonging. They support, uplift, and inspire us as we face life's obstacles.

Therefore, maintaining good connections can positively impact not only ourselves but also the people around us and have a profound effect on numerous facets of our lives. By adhering to Islamic principles, Muslims can build and maintain healthy, supportive relationships.

Individuals from different cultural origins, races, and faiths collaborate to achieve shared objectives in a workplace that is becoming more globalised and varied. These people include Muslim professionals who deal with particular difficulties in their work. These difficulties may occasionally impede their professional development and achievement.

Comprehending these difficulties is essential to creating an inclusive and encouraging work environment where everyone can succeed. Let's examine some of the major issues that Muslim professionals face and how they should respond to them in accordance with Islamic guidelines.

Work-Life Balance

Islam fully supports leading a balanced life. The below verse indicates that Muslims have been instructed to embrace balance in all spheres of life, including employment, family, and all other areas.

"Thus have We made you the people of the middle."
(Quran 2:144)

For every one of us, finding a good work-life balance is a constant battle. Being Muslim presents us with special obstacles that might leave us feeling overwhelmed and frustrated in ourselves for not doing enough to maintain balance in all facets of our lives. These challenges stem from our obligations to family, community, education, health, and, most importantly, Allah (SWT).

We are constantly faced with challenges in life that prevent us from managing and leading genuinely balanced lives. You may be convinced at this point that it is impossible to achieve a work-life balance! Now is a good time to reflect on the lessons from the life and practices of our Prophet Muhammad (PBUH).

Lessons from Prophet Muhammad (PBUH)

As Muslims, we cannot overlook how well-balanced and efficient Prophet Muhammad's (PBUH) daily schedule was throughout his life. In just 23 years, He (PBUH) altered the course of human history. There are invaluable lessons from his life that we can apply to our own lives.

One of the Prophet's (PBUH) companions, Abdullah ibn Amr ibn al-As (RA), reportedly fasted and prayed all day and night. The Prophet Muhammad (PBUH) said: "I have been informed that you fast during the day and stand in prayer all night." I replied, "Yes, I do." He said, "Do not do that. Fast and break your fast; stand in prayer and sleep."

"For your eyes have a right over you, your body has a right over you, your body has a right over you, your wife has a right over you, your guest has a right over you, and your friend has a right over you..." (Sahih Bukhari)

We should view work-life balance in terms of upholding our rights—the rights of our bodies, minds, families, friends, and, of course, our workplaces—rather than what other people expect of us. This is the most important lesson this situation teaches us.

It becomes incredibly obvious and straightforward where to draw the line between the many aspects of our lives and how to balance them given the circumstances once we change how we think about work-life balance from subjective/idealistic conceptions to the rights of others (and ourselves).

Moreover, work-life balance isn't just about allocating our time; it's about being fully present wherever we are. By focusing on fulfilling our rights and responsibilities and being engaged in the moment, we can achieve true balance in life.

The Prophet Muhammad's (PBUH) life teaches us the importance of living a balanced life by fulfilling the rights of our bodies, minds, and relationships. We can achieve true harmony by shifting our focus from work-life balance to upholding these rights. His (PBUH) example guides us in balancing the various aspects of our lives effectively.

Ethical Dilemmas

Ethical dilemmas are very common in workplace settings. False accounting, data privacy, nepotism, sexual harassment and discrimination are just a few examples of the ethical difficulties that arise in today's workplace. An ethical dilemma is a paradox that occurs when two or more options exist, but none is the best ethical or moral option.

Islam provides clear guidelines for Muslims to uphold ethical standards in these challenging situations. Islam's ethical framework is explained in the context of Shariah. This Islamic social and legal code holds that anything that promotes the welfare of a person or community is morally right, and anything that harms others is morally wrong.

Islam promotes the concept of justice, fairness and trustworthiness as moral conduct.

> *The Holy Prophet (PBUH) said, "Leave that which makes you doubt for that which does not make you doubt, for truthfulness is certainty and tranquillity, while falsehood is doubt and confusion." (Tirmidhi)*

Career Advancement

Muslims must consider Islam when making a career decision. Choosing a job route simply because it is financially rewarding, widely accepted, or that everyone else appears to be following is not the ideal approach.

For us as Muslims, choosing the right career path is crucial since it will have an impact on our productivity. It also has the power to make or ruin our afterlife in addition to our earthly existence. Pursuing career growth that best aligns with Islamic values can be challenging.

But as Muslims, we are bound to select a career option that is strictly Halal. Our ultimate goal is to please Allah (SWT) at all times when making employment decisions. Therefore, we must pursue avenues that allow us to hold fast to the Islamic teachings of the Quran and hadith.

These paths not only ensure we are rewarded for our good deeds but also turn our efforts into acts of worship. By earning through Halal means and using that income in Halal ways, particularly to support ourselves and our families, we elevate our work to a spiritual level.

Since Allah (SWT) Himself is a witness to our transactions, we are obligated to act in an Islamic manner when conducting business:

"In whatever business you may be, and whatever portion you may be reciting from the Quran and whatever deed you may be doing, We are Witnesses thereof when you are deeply engrossed therein." (Quran 10:61)

The Prophet (PBUH) said, "Truthfulness leads to righteousness, and righteousness leads to Paradise. A man continues to tell the truth until he becomes a truthful person. Falsehood leads to al fujuwr (i.e. wickedness, evil-doing), and al fujuwr (wickedness) leads to the (Hell) Fire, and a man may continue to tell lies till he is written before Allah (SWT), a liar." (Sahih Bukhari)

Spiritual Spherc

Distress and perceived progress have been linked to religious and spiritual challenges, characterised as conflict or tension surrounding religious and spiritual practices, beliefs, or experiences. Let's examine some typical obstacles Muslims encounter on their path to get closer to Allah (SWT).

Consistency in Worship

There is more to our journey to Allah (SWT) than just a physical one. In Islam, the heart is the most important organ. We know and love Allah Almighty with all of our hearts.

The Prophet Muhammad (PBUH) says that if the heart is good, then the state of the believer will be good, and if the heart is corrupt, so too will be one's state. (Sahih Bukhari)

At times, we consciously set out on the path to Allah (SWT) and find it effortless to remain on course. Sometimes, though, we become distracted. We become disheartened, gazing forward and thinking we might not succeed. This is often because the spiritual journey can be challenging.

Our challenges lies in becoming so anaesthetised by the worldly humankind around us and our own whims and desires that our hearts become covered up, blinded to the reality of Allah's (SWT) nearness. Thus, we stray, make mistakes, and harden our hearts, making it harder to distinguish between what is beautiful and ugly, between truth and deception.

For instance, maintaining regularity in our daily worship practices—such as offering five times prayer (Salah), fasting (Sawm), and giving acts of charity—can be challenging, especially amidst a busy lifestyle. However, hope remains. Just keep in mind that consistency is essential for spiritual growth. It would be prudent for us to gradually improve and draw nearer to Allah (SWT). We should start by improving one thing and sticking with it rather than trying to fix everything at once.

There is a well-known hadith of the Prophet Muhammad (PBUH) that reflects this principle. He (PBUH) said Allah (SWT) says: "My servant does not draw near to Me with anything more beloved to Me than what I have obligated upon him. My servant continues to draw near to Me with the voluntary acts until I love him. Once I love him, I am his hearing with which he hears, his sight with which he sees, his hand with which he grasps, and his foot with which he walks. Were he to ask of Me, I would surely grant it to him. If he were to seek refuge with Me, I would surely protect him." (Sahih Bukhari)

This hadith clearly outlines the priorities that a Muslim should have when moving towards Allah (SWT). As true believers, we must consistently carry out the required acts of worship that Allah (SWT) has decreed, such as the conviction that Allah (SWT) is one, the five daily prayers, the Ramadan fast, the required almsgiving, and the Hajj. It is our duty to follow what Allah (SWT) has approved and to stay away from what He has forbidden.

Our goals should be to grow as individuals and rid our hearts of spiritual illnesses. The Prophet's (PBUH) companions, many of whom continued to follow this supererogatory act of worship until the day of their deaths, did so when they were drawn to it.

> *Allah (SWT) says: "And worship your Lord until there comes to you the certainty (death)." (Quran 15:99)*

This verse should inspire us to remain steadfast in our worship and devotion. As we commit to our improvements, other aspects of our lives will become easier. Allah (SWT) will pave the way for us as long as we keep going forward and truly repent of the mistakes we shall unavoidably commit.

> *Allah (SWT) says: "And (as for) those who strive hard for Us, We will most certainly guide them in our ways; and Allah (SWT) is most surely with the doers of good." (Quran 29:69)*

Strengthening Faith

Islam's view of faith is fundamental to what it means to be a Muslim. It situates us within what may be called a "belief framework," which grows into a way of life and offers a special logic system of its own to explain the phenomena of the world around us.

We may be grateful for the favours we have received and patient throughout trying times because we believe that nothing happens without Allah's (SWT) will. According to the Quran, some people need to see something physical or visible.

Regularly engaging with the Quran and participating in community activities can enhance understanding and reinforce faith. Islam also emphasises the importance of surrounding oneself with supportive, like-minded individuals who can provide encouragement and guidance.

Balancing Material and Spiritual Life

It's quite difficult to strike a balance between material possessions and Islamic spiritual development. The Quran seems to have a recurring theme in which Allah (SWT) uses two types of people as examples: those who have dedicated their time and energy to worldly and material pursuits, and others who have "abandoned" the material world and decided to distance themselves from life's hardships.

This is evident from the Quran's first Surah. At least seventeen times a day, Muslims recite Surat al-Fatiha, which says, "Guide us to the straight path - The path of those upon with which You have bestowed favour, not of those who have evoked (Your) contempt or of those who are astray."

In essence, every person exists on a spectrum, with the pursuit of the material at one end and the pursuit of the spiritual at the other. Whether they realise it or not, this balance affects all individuals. One of the best examples in Islamic history of someone who harmonised the material and spirituality is the Prophet Muhammad (PBUH).

He guided Muslims and served as both the supreme commander and the Imam. Because he believed in the combined strength of the material and spiritual realms, he placed his Ummah in the middle of the previously indicated scale. Of course, the closest relationship with Allah (SWT) was that of the Prophet (PBUH). His highest spiritual endeavour was to recite and meditate on the Quran.

On a personal level, a Muslim needs to balance these extremes and maintain vigilance. Without going too far, materialism is necessary and a feature of the human experience. This also holds true for spirituality, which is attained by sincere adherence to the teachings of the Quran and the prophets.

Thus, navigating personal, professional, and spiritual challenges through an Islamic lens involves integrating religious principles with daily life. By following the guidance provided in the Quran and the Hadith, Muslims can address these challenges effectively, fostering a harmonious and fulfilling life that aligns with their religious principles.

Understanding the purpose of tests and hardships in the Islamic worldview

This planet is sometimes referred to in the Islamic worldview as "Dar al-Bala," which translates to "the abode of trials." This idea is essential to comprehending life from an Islamic viewpoint because it stresses how difficult life on earth may be and how it tests our faith.

In life, we will always experience ups and downs, and sometimes, it seems like our struggles will never stop. Numerous verses in the Quran mention the various ways Allah (SWT) will test us, but He also gives us a care package to get us through those difficult times. The purpose of these trials is to test our willingness to obey the commands of Allah (SWT).

Unaware of the reasons for hardships, people may begin to believe that life is unfair or even that Allah (SWT) is unjust. However, Allah (SWT) is Al-Adl (The Just) and Al-Rahman (The Most Merciful). He only desires the best for us and never wishes harm to His people. The

Quran and Hadith include a wealth of information that enables us to respond to why we are tested.

Allah's (SWT) prophets experienced extreme adversity, as you will discover if you read about their lives. One of Allah's (SWT) unchanging and all-encompassing principles is that He will put someone to the test in this world when He loves them.

> *Allah (SWT) says in the Quran: "Do the people think that they will be left to say, "We believe" and they will not be tried? But we have certainly tried those before them, and Allah (SWT) will surely make evident those who are truthful, and He will surely make evident those who are false." (Quran 29:2-3)*

> *"And most certainly shall We try you by means of danger, and hunger, and loss of worldly goods, of lives and of labour's fruits. But give glad tidings unto those who are patient in adversity" (Quran 2:155)*

Therefore, it is truly a magnificent gift if He takes away a person's worldly existence, or a portion of it, and leads him to repentance, offering Him grace and Paradise in its place!

> *The Prophet (PBUH) said: "No calamity befalls a Muslim but that Allah expiates some of his sins because of it, even if it were the prick of a thorn." (Bukhari & Muslim)*

So, to purify us and erase our sins, Allah (SWT) puts us through trials. Hence, rather than viewing tests as a means of punishing us, this indicates that Allah's (SWT) intention is to deliver us from punishment—that is, the punishment that awaits us in the Hereafter, which is far harsher than any test we will ever encounter in this life.

In addition to this, Allah (SWT) puts us through trials to refine and strengthen us as Muslims. When you successfully pass a test, you become a different person.

You are more confident in Allah (SWT), more equipped to face challenges in the future, and more optimistic about your chances of success.

> *The Prophet (PBUH) said the extent of the reward will be in accordance with the extent of the trial. If Allah (SWT) loves a people, He tries them, and whoever is content will have contentment, and whoever is angry will have anger. (Tirmidhi)*

Remind yourself to remain patient whenever a trial arises. If exercising patience is hard for you, start by simply acting patient; over time, the act will transform into true patience. The best course of action is to simply remain silent and ask Allah (SWT) for patience.

> *The Prophet (PBUH) said that real patience is at the first stroke of a calamity. (Sahih Bukhari)*

In the Islamic worldview, tests and hardships are seen as purposeful and essential aspects of life. They refine the believer's character, purify their soul, and strengthen their faith.

By enduring these trials with patience, trust in Allah (SWT), and a focus on the Hereafter, Muslims believe they can achieve spiritual growth and attain the ultimate success of pleasing Allah (SWT) and earning a place in Paradise.

<u>Importance of Resilience and Perseverance in Adversity</u>

Islam offers a comprehensive framework for finding comfort, support, and direction during trying times. Whether confronted with personal difficulties, social turmoil, or international disasters, followers of Islam seek solace and illumination from the teachings of the faith.

Islam strongly emphasises resilience and perseverance, particularly in the face of adversity. Resilience is the ability to rise above hardship and endure it. It's a common misconception that resilience means you can't feel anxious or angry when things are tough.

Even when a negative event causes you to feel hurt, angry, and sad, you can still move on. These feelings are natural, and resilience lies in the capacity to bounce back from setbacks and adjust to tough life circumstances with an unyielding spirit.

When faced with such obstacles, resilient people demonstrate an incredible ability to recover, adjust, and become stronger. As a tribute to the human spirit and our inherent power, resilience enables us to harness our inner strength to overcome obstacles and serves as a constant reminder that even in the darkest of circumstances, there is hope and light.

The continuous endeavour to perform or accomplish anything in the face of obstacles, setbacks, or resistance is known as perseverance. It is the resilient spirit that leads us through life, enabling us to overcome challenges and achieve extraordinary feats.

People who persevere have unwavering faith in their own abilities, as well as in their vision or goals. Perseverance empowers us to rise to challenges and learn from them, never letting failures define who we are. Despite any challenges we may have faced, perseverance lights a fire within us and drives us ahead.

Perseverance and resilience build a powerful combination that helps people navigate life's challenges. Perseverance gives people the unshakeable willpower to move forward, while resilience gives them the skills necessary to gracefully adjust to unexpected events.

People who are able to balance these qualities are better able to live meaningful, fulfilling lives. Resilience is the thread connecting adaptability to determination in the intricate fabric of existence. Together, they create a masterpiece that is braided with strands of courage, strength, and unflinching resolve—a story of triumph over adversity.

Here are some essential guidelines and steps that Islam prescribes for getting through trying times:

Islam strongly emphasises the idea of Tawakkul or dependence on Allah (SWT). Muslims are instructed to submit their matters to Allah (SWT), realising He is the ultimate source of direction and strength. This faith gives consolation during trying times because it acknowledges that Allah (SWT) is the best disposer of all affairs.

Islam places a strong emphasis on gaining knowledge as a path to empowerment and enlightenment. Muslims are urged to seek wisdom during trying times by studying the Quran, the Hadith (the sayings of the Prophet Muhammad PBUH), and consulting respectable scholars. Individuals can acquire perspective, discernment, and direction through knowledge, enabling them to effectively handle obstacles.

In Islam, difficult circumstances present opportunities for reflection and personal development. Believers are recommended to reflect on their actions, ask for pardon for previous transgressions, and work towards personal development. By exercising self-control, confessing one's sins, and upholding moral standards, individuals can become stronger and more spiritually sensitive to Allah's (SWT) direction.

The Prophet (PBUH) experienced several challenging periods in his personal and communal life. Even while his life was the most successful, it was also the most difficult. With the help of Allah's (SWT) will and guidance, he overcame all obstacles and emerged stronger from the dark periods than before.

Embracing Challenges as Opportunities for Growth

The Islamic teachings emphasise that life's trials are opportunities for true Muslims to prove their commitment to Allah (SWT) and to grow spiritually.

We can use the words of the Quran to adopt an alternative viewpoint, one in which suffering is Allah's (SWT) way of putting our faith to the test and providing us with the chance to mature rather than viewing it as punishment.

"Allah (SWT) does not charge a soul except [with that within] its capacity. It will have [the consequence of] what [good] it has gained, and it will bear [the consequence of] what [evil] it has earned..." (Quran 2:286)

Therefore, every challenge and adversity is precisely what your faith needs to strengthen. Not any more, not any less.

These tests are designed to bring forth the inner strength, resilience, and dependence of the believers on Allah (SWT), not to cause harm or suffering.

Through these hardships, believers have the chance to show their trust in Allah's (SWT) knowledge and benevolence, as well as to ask for His direction and assistance. Through these trials, believers can better comprehend the depth of their faith and forge a closer bond with their Creator.

Thus, tests are given to believers to sharpen their faith and deepen their relationship with Allah (SWT), much like fire purifies gold and silver. Believers have the chance to show that they trust in Allah's (SWT) wisdom and ask for His guidance through these hardships. Knowing that the eternal happiness of Paradise is our ultimate reward, may we all endeavour to stay patient and steady in the face of misfortune.

Allah (SWT) is, after all, with those who have whole faith in Him and remain patient. We have to submit to His divine plan because it is His will. He may be bestowing a favour onto us covertly, in addition to having the last say.

It is reassuring to know that the tests we face and the rewards we receive are proportional to our level of faith. When difficulties arise, we ought to view them as a chance for immense happiness. Testing our faith allows us to strengthen our endurance.

We ought to let it flourish because, once our endurance is fully re-alised, we will be whole and perfect. We will only require this faith to sustain us as we pursue Allah's (SWT) plan and eventually arrive at our true destination—the Hereafter.

Remember that sometimes the greatest act of faith is to just rise from the dust and face another day, acknowledging that Islam is nothing more than surrendering to God's will.

Chapter Three

Trusting in Divine Decree (Qadr)

Concept of Qadr (Divine Decree) in Islam

In Islam, the idea of divine decree, or Qadr, refers to the conviction that the cosmos and everything in it are the product of Allah's (SWT) all-encompassing and predetermined plan.

Muslims hold that everything, including events, results, and each person's fate, is completely within the knowledge and power of Allah (SWT), the One who created and sustains the entire universe.

One of the six pillars of religion, as stated by the Prophet (PBUH), is belief in Al-Qadr. The Prophet (PBUH) made this statement in response to Hazrat Jibril's (AS) question concerning faith (Iman).

He said: "(It is) to believe in Allah (SWT), His angels, His Books, His Messengers, the Last Day, and to believe in the Divine will and decree (al-qadr) both good and bad." (Sahih Muslim)

The Arabic term Qadr denotes planning and evaluation, respectively, and perfection and completeness. Within the Islamic language, Qadr refers to Allah's (SWT) predetermined plan for everything from the beginning of time, as well as His awareness that these plans will materialise just as He has intended and ordered. They will transpire in the manner in which they are intended to be generated.

Allah (SWT) states about Al-Qadar: "Verily, We have created all things with Qadr" (Quran 54:49)

For Muslims, understanding and embracing Qadr is integral to their faith, as it underscores the omnipotence of Allah (SWT) and the finite understanding of humankind.

It is narrated that Ibn 'Umar (RA) heard that some people were denying al-qadr. He said: "If I meet these people, I will tell them that I have nothing to do with them, and they have nothing to do with me. By the One by Whom 'Abd-Allah ibn 'Umar swore, if one of them had gold equivalent to Mount Uhud and he spent it, Allah (SWT) would not accept it from him unless he believed in al-qadr." (Sahih Muslim)

Understanding predestination and free will within the framework of Islamic belief

Predestination is the belief that all that occurs has already been predetermined by Allah (SWT) and that nothing occurs unless it is in accordance with His will.

This does not imply, however, that people are not free to choose. Rather, it indicates that Allah (SWT) is aware of people's choices.

Predestination, sometimes known as fate, is a notion commonly misinterpreted or confused with the doctrines of other philosophies or religions.

Words like fate, destiny, divine decision, and predestination are frequently used without any kind of clarification or distinction. Muslims must comprehend the term Qadr, which is used in Arabic.

The Prophet Muhammad (PBUH) said, "No servant of Allah (SWT) will truly believe until he believes in al-qadr, its good and bad, until he knows that what afflicted him could never miss him, and that what missed him could never have afflicted him." (Tirmidhi)

If our faith requires us to accept Qadr—the good and the terrible, the sweet and the bitter—then it is critical that we comprehend some fundamental ideas that each and every Muslim should be aware of.

The Four Facets of Al-Qadr (Divine Decree) Belief

- **Knowledge (Ilm)**

The fact that Allah (SWT) is All-Knowing is the first fundamental truth we must accept. Past, present, and future are all known to him. Allah (SW) is also aware of every alternative that could have existed, including the consequences of picking a different course in life, a different profession, or any other option.

The conviction that everything that occurs in this cosmos, no matter how big or small, is covered by Allah's (SWT) understanding, all of Allah's (SWT) activities and the actions of His servants are included in His Knowledge.

The Quran states: "And with Him are the keys of the unseen; none knows them except Him. And He knows what is on the land and in the sea. Not a leaf falls but that He knows it. And no grain is there within the darknesses of the earth and no moist or dry [thing] but that it is [written] in a clear record." (Quran 6:59)

He is fully knowledgeable about all facets and details of life. Before the universe was established, Allah (SWT) was aware of every detail, including lifespans, deeds, and speech, aware of who would follow the straight road and who would take the wrong one, as well as who among them would seek out Paradise and who would deserve to suffer punishment in the Hereafter.

As Muslims it is necessary for us to believe that from eternity to eternity, Allah (SWT) is aware of everything, both generally and specifically. He is aware of every particle in the earth and the heavens.

- **Writing (Kitabah)**

Belief in Allah's (SWT) recording of everything prior to the creation of the earth and the heavens constitutes the second level of belief in Qadr.

It is crucial to understand that once the All-Knowing's incredible wisdom has been acknowledged, all that Allah (SWT) knew about the creation of the world and all that was to occur in it is recorded in the 'Al-Lawh Al-Mahfooth', sometimes known as "The Preserved Tablet."

Allah (SWT) says: "Do you not know that Allah (SWT) knows what is in the heaven and earth? Indeed that is in a Record [i.e., Al-Lawh Al-Mahfooth]. Indeed that, for Allah, is easy." (Quran 22:70)

The Prophet Muhammad (PBUH) said: "Allah Almighty has written down the decrees of creation fifty thousand years before He created the heavens and the earth." (Sahih Muslim)

Simply put, Allah (SWT) knew all that would transpire during creation and all that we would eventually learn about our last destinations as well. This information was recorded in a preserved area.

- **Will (Mashiah)**

The third step is to accept that everything that exists is predetermined by Allah (SWT) and that nothing can exist if He does not will it to.

Again, everything is included in this. It alludes to the deeds that humans commit as well as Allah's (SWT) actions of providing life, nourishment, and other things. Nothing can be done unless Allah (SWT) wills it to happen.

"And your Lord creates what He wills and chooses..." (Quran 28:68) And "...And Allah (SWT) does what He wills." (Quran 14:27) And "It is He who forms you in the wombs however He wills..." (Quran 3:6) As for actions taken by His creation, Allah (SWT) Says: "...And if Allah (SWT) had willed, He could have given them power over you, and they would have fought you." (Quran 4:90)

"...And if Allah (SWT) had willed, they would not have done so. So leave them and that which they invent." (Quran 6:137)

Many people have a serious misconception regarding what is meant to be Allah's (SWT) will. They interpret it to suggest that what is agreeable to Allah (SWT) is also what He wishes to happen in the cosmos.

However, that is not what we Muslims believe. We believe that Allah (SWT), as He tells us, likes certain things and hates others, but because of His wisdom, He made this world of trials and free will choices—a world that is easy and difficult, sweet and bitter.

Furthermore, either eternal happiness or eternal condemnation comes before this life, this test. Although Allah (SWT) grants us free will to make decisions, He detests when people reject what is right or the truth.

He says, "And Allah (SWT) does not like for His servants to disbelieve." (Quran 39:7)

Yet many individuals have heard the truth and freely choose not to believe. He has told us to "do not oppress," yet he also gives people the freedom to oppress others while issuing a dire warning about the retribution that awaits those who choose to oppress others in the hereafter.

Muslims consider the ability to select one's actions as part of free will. The reason Allah (SWT) knows what you will pick in advance is because He is not constrained by time, place, or anything else. Because he is omniscient, he knows everything about the choices you and I make in our lifetimes before we were even created.

This is not the same as being created and then predestined (compelled or otherwise programmed, either intrinsically or externally) to select a path of disobedience or wicked deeds without having the ability to exercise free choice. Actually, under Islam, you are not even held responsible for actions that you take because of the actions of other people (e.g., someone compelled to utter something offensive at gunpoint). Only your free will holds you responsible.

You have both significant and minor decisions in daily life. You make decisions about how to live your life, how to handle adversity, and whether to make the most of the Creator's blessings, such as time and health.

You also make decisions about how you react to the world around you. You will only be held responsible for those decisions on the Day of Judgement because they are all matters of choice.

Your free will determines both your good deeds and your crimes. You are responsible for your decisions; Allah (SWT) is knowledgeable, and you have a choice.

Allah's (SWT) will is the force behind every occurrence in the universe. While humans make choices, these choices and their consequences are ultimately within the scope of Allah's (SWT) will.

- **Creation (Khalq)**

The idea that Allah (SWT) created, brought into being, and made everything exist constitutes the fourth stage of Qadar belief. Numerous verses in the Quran also illustrate this point, including:

Allah (SWT) says: "Allah is the Creator of all things, and He is, over all things, Disposer of affairs." (Quran 39:62)

"...He has created each thing and determined it with [precise] determination." (Quran: 25:2) Also, Hazrat Ibraheem (AS) said to his people: "While Allah created you and that which you do?" (Quran 37:96)

Some enquire as to whether faith in divine decree (Qadr) deprives one of life's purpose while, in actuality, the contrary is true. A belief in Qadr highlights the significance of life, the weight of one's decisions, and the idea that one is living for a higher, eternal purpose.

Belief in Qadr has a psychological and emotional impact on us because it satisfies our need for transcendence in life, encourages us to persevere through adversity, aids in the healing process after tragic events, and offers resilience and perseverance to those who seek it. This belief shields us from the pointless, ordinary lifestyles of today's materialists and nihilists.

The interplay between predestination and free will in Islam is a complex yet coherent doctrine that shapes the beliefs and practices of believers. It acknowledges Allah's (SWT) absolute sovereignty while affirming human responsibility and accountability.

This balance offers a unique perspective on life, one that encourages proactive living while trusting in the divine wisdom of Allah's (SWT) decree. For Muslims, understanding and embracing this balance is essential for a fulfilling and meaningful life.

Strengthening faith (Iman) by trusting Allah's wisdom and plan for our lives

In Islam, faith (Iman) is more than just belief; it's a profound trust in Allah's (SWT) wisdom and His divine plan for our lives. This trust forms the foundation of a Muslim's relationship with Allah (SWT) and is essential for spiritual growth and resilience.

The Quran and Sunnah offer Muslims comfort and direction in trying times. Islam holds that life is a passing test and that adversity can help us become our best selves, develop our religion, and atone for our sins.

Islam teaches us to see this world as our temporary home, where Allah (SWT) tests His people solely to strengthen their faith when it falters, to atone for their transgressions, and to bring out the best in each of them. In times of hardship, Muslims must refer to these tools found within the intricate web of Islamic teachings.

Believing in Allah's (SWT) plan among life's complex patterns of happiness and sorrow is a fundamental aspect of Islam. Tawakkul, or trust, is an expression of deep faith and dependence on Allah's (SWT) knowledge and benevolence.

Amid life's uncertainty, this spiritual practice offers comfort, strength, and a sense of purpose.

Trust is an active state of faith that combines dependence on Allah (SWT) with the endeavour to make the right decisions and do the necessary acts. It is not a passive faith.

Tawakkul is the recognition that although we must work hard and strive, Allah (SWT) has the final say and that His wisdom is above our understanding.

When we have faith in His plan, our objectives and deeds are in line with Allah's (SWT) will. This congruence gives us direction and clarity, enabling us to make morally and religiously sound decisions. It affirms that we are here to worship Allah (SWT) and make beneficial contributions to the world.

> *"So when you have decided, then rely upon Allah. Indeed, Allah loves those who rely [upon Him]." (Quran 3:159)*

Trusting in Allah's (SWT) wisdom and plan is a cornerstone of faith (Iman). It is through this trust that we find the strength to navigate life's ups and downs, knowing that everything unfolds according to Allah's (SWT) perfect plan.

Coping with Unexpected Circumstances and Uncertainty

Making decisions is inevitable in life. We make decisions every minute of the day, some unimportant and others more significant.

We yearn to know if each decision we make is the right course of action before committing to anything. Because knowing something is certain makes us feel secure and in control of our lives.

But we must always keep in mind that we don't always have control over events. For everyone, uncertainty is a normal aspect of existence. Allah (SWT) is the sole unchanging entity in the cosmos; as He states, "Everything will perish except His Facc." Allah (SWT) informs us that the most important matters in this life are solely under His certainty and control.

Compared to someone who constantly craves control and certainty, a person who can endure uncertainty and feel comfortable with it tends to navigate life more effectively. This ability allows them to focus on what they can control without being overwhelmed by things beyond their control.

On the other hand, the person who flees from uncertainty and craves control over their life's specifics will discover that "what they resist to persist." They will always be in a condition of anxiety, worry, and stress and find only ambiguity everywhere.

People who experience uncertainty and a sense of being powerless tend to react negatively by becoming stressed.

The Islamic perspective urges us to put our energy and attention where we have the most control and to give Allah (SWT) authority over the things over which we have no control.

The Prophet (PBUH) beautifully explained this: "Were you to put your complete trust in Allah (SWT), He would provide for you as He provides for the birds. They go out hungry in the morning and return filled in the evening." (Tirmidhi)

When the birds leave their nests early in the morning, they have no idea when, where, or what they will catch. Yet, this uncertainty does not paralyse them; instead, it spurs them on to do the one thing within their power: genuinely seek out what has been predetermined for them. Likewise, with regard to facets of life over which the Prophet (PBUH) had no influence and could not predict the result, he would offer dua (such as istikhara) to Allah (SWT) and proceed.

Allah (SWT) is wise in all that He does, and He will test people according to how they handle this uncertainty. Our objective, then, is to ascertain what elements of an adaptive mindset make us eligible to be included in the patient population.

Develop Wisdom (Hikma) in Uncertain Times

The capacity to recognise the beauty and significance in all that occurs in our lives is known as hikma, or wisdom from Allah (SWT). Al Hakeem, the All-Wise, is one of Allah's (SWT) names. We can live more clearly and optimistically when we put our faith in His Wisdom and apply the lessons He has revealed in His Book (Quran) to everything.

Allah (SWT) says: "The Most Compassionate, Taught the Quran. He created human beings, and taught him speech." (Quran 55:1-4)

Notably, Allah (SWT) stated that He "taught the Quran" before mentioning the creation or the development of human intelligence. The Quran provides humanity with the highest level of intelligence and direction, enabling them to navigate life's ups and downs with greater grace.

The knowledge found in the Quran encompasses not only intellectual intelligence, or "Aql," but also spiritual intelligence found in heart-based faith and direction. Al Hakeem, or "the wise book," is one term used to characterise the Quran. The Quran was revealed by Allah (SWT), the All-Wise, to impart wisdom to us. So, this kind of intelligence is essential to our achievement.

> *Allah says: "Ya, Seen By the Quran rich in wisdom."*
> *(Quran 36:1-2)*

Through the Divine teachings to His chosen messengers, whom He commanded to instruct and reflect His Hikma to people, Allah (SWT) revealed the ultimate wisdom or understanding.

> *Allah (SWT) told Prophet Muhammad (PBUH): "Invite*
> *to the way of your Lord with Hikma and kind teaching."*
> *(Quran 16:125)*

Allah (SWT) ordered the Prophet Muhammad (PBUH) to employ the quality of hikma to convey assurance during life's uncertainties, lead the lost, and resurrect dead hearts. The Beloved Prophet (PBUH) was the epitome of wisdom in his life, handling all the difficulties and doubts he encountered when he began calling people to Allah's (SWT) way.

He also required a great degree of knowledge when attempting to revive barren souls. "Hikma, or Wisdom from Allah (SWT), is the capacity to recognise the worth and significance of every experience we have in life. We can become more positive and clear-headed when we put our trust in His Wisdom.

Finding solace in accepting Allah's decree during challenging times

As Muslims, we believe that everything in our lives is according to Allah's (SWT) will and wisdom, which provides us comfort and resilience.

As we are battling with our flaws, hardships, and relationships, the chaos can cause our hearts to vacillate between feeling overwhelmed and numb. In these turbulent times, how should we react? With all the suffering that is going on, how are we supposed to stay hopeful?

Allah (SWT) reminds us that we will be put to the test by hardships, so we must be spiritually strong and persistent to be ready for these unforeseen circumstances. When we learn about an impending exam at school, we are inherently more mentally prepared, which motivates us to take the necessary steps to succeed.

It's like preparing ourselves for the blows of life's volatility. As a result, we must prepare ourselves mentally for impending adversity by concentrating on overcoming it with acceptance and patience.

Even when put through trying and painful experiences, we must have the maturity and awareness to recognise that these experiences are helping us learn important lessons and advance spiritually.

As the Holy Prophet (PBUH) said: "The strong believer is better and more beloved to Allah (SWT) than the weak believer, while there is good in both. Strive for that which will benefit you, seek the help of Allah (SWT), and do not feel helpless. If anything befalls you, do not say, 'If only I had done such and such.' Rather say (Allah SWT decreed, and what He wills, He does).' For indeed, saying 'If' opens the doors to the deeds of Satan." (Sahih Muslim)

These teachings encourage acceptance of Allah's (SWT) will and reliance on His wisdom, bringing peace to the heart during trials. Acceptance of our fate, our past, and our present is the path to ultimate serenity. We can more easily accept suffering when we acknowledge that everything that has taken place for us and is happening now has been planned by Allah (SWT). We can do this when we are confident that events do not occur randomly and that divine wisdom is at play in our lives.

> *The Holy Prophet (PBUH) said: "How amazing is the affair of the believer. There is good for him in everything and that is for no one but the believer. If good times come his way, he expresses gratitude to Allah (SWT) and that is good for him, and if hardship comes his way, he endures it patiently and that is better for him." (Sahih Muslim)*

We learn to be more patient when acknowledging that the challenges serve a wise and meaningful purpose. It's comparable to a medical student who, despite the long hours of study, sleep deprivation, and strenuous effort, remains steadfast, knowing that short-term hardship ultimately results in long-term achievement. Our hearts will overflow with hope when we fully believe in Allah (SWT), knowing that everything we go through will change us and that patience will be rewarded.

Having reached a condition of mental preparedness, acceptance, and nurturing confidence in Allah (SWT), we shall naturally possess an optimistic disposition and state of mind. Understanding that nothing is permanent requires us to bring hope into our despair. The suffering and challenges we are currently facing will ultimately pass. Even though it might be difficult to see the light at the end of the tunnel, if we concentrate on achieving one tiny goal at a time, we can gradually grow hope in our hearts and emerge from the shadows.

Developing inner peace through surrendering to the Divine will

The secret to this metamorphosis is surrender, which allows divine power to refine, purify, and transform the individual. Through submission, the ego vanishes, making way for a higher, divine consciousness, a sense of inner harmony, serenity, and oneness with the Divine.

Allah's (SWT) decision might be compared to a stage in life, a degree of faith, or an explanation for how and why things occur. It occurs when you recognise that everything in your life is a gift from Allah (SWT) and are completely happy and content with all that is thrown at you.

Whether it's something you adore, something you hope will happen again, something you're not so sure about, something you'd rather avoid, or something you wish would never return, you embrace and find satisfaction in all that you receive!

So, to reach this stage and degree of contentment, we must practise Shukr (gratitude) during our happiest moments. Through our worship and supplications, we should express our thankfulness and appreciation to Allah (SWT) for all that we have. Equally important is Sabr (patience) during difficult times. The One who hears all we say is Allah (SWT), so we must turn to Him. We must be open about our shortcomings and grieve Him. We must earnestly ask for what we desire.

We must recognise that everything occurs for a purpose, and that purpose is the result of Allah's (SWT) decree. It's possible that Allah (SWT) observes our reactions and behaviours during these times. Will we turn to Him, seeking to grow closer to Him, or will we lose faith in the One in whom all hope is found?

Therefore, whether a gift is a blessing or a challenge, if we truly love Allah (SWT), we will adore everything He provides us.

Chapter Four

Building Spiritual Resilience

Strengthening Spiritual Foundations for Resilience

These days, suffering is accepted as a normal part of existence. To respond appropriately and manage it effectively, we must adopt suitable measures. Spirituality, with its long history and ongoing relevance in psychology, plays a crucial role in fostering resilience, personal development, and overall well-being.

The capacity to overcome suffering, adjust to change, and preserve mental health in the face of adversity is known as resilience. For a lot of Muslims, perseverance and mental health are greatly aided by their religion in Islam.

The Quran encourages Muslims to apply their intelligence, or "Aql," to solve difficulties that arise in their daily lives. The Quran repeatedly emphasises and repeats specific words to remind and uplift them to be imaginative and mindful of their wants and well-being.

Islam promotes resilience among Muslims as a means of achieving peace in life. From an Islamic perspective, resilience includes a range of qualities, including flexibility, the ability to learn from events, optimism and self-belief, self-control over appetites, empathy, reliability and accountability.

> *Prophet Muhammad (PBUH) said: The example of a believer is that of a fresh tender plant; from whatever direction the wind comes, it bends it, but when the wind becomes quiet, it becomes straight again. Similarly, a believer is afflicted with calamities (but he remains patient till Allah removes his difficulties). And an impious wicked person is like a cedar tree that stays hard and straight till Allah cuts (breaks) it down when He wishes. (Sahih Bukhari)*

This hadith demonstrates how resilience can help us strengthen and preserve our relationship with Allah (SWT) in difficult circumstances and how its absence can obstruct that ability.

Spiritual activities in Islamic psychology are based on the Islamic teachings and customs of the Prophet Muhammad (PBUH). Such acts primarily foster psychological health, inner serenity, and a stronger bond with the Almighty Allah (SWT). You can strengthen your spiritual ties and become more resilient during trying times by engaging in these practices. Let's have a look at it!

Cultivating Taqwa as a source of inner strength

Many translations of the Arabic term "Taqwa" indicate "piety or righteousness," "fear of Allah (SWT)," "obedience to Allah (SWT)," "self-restraint," and "refraining from sinful act(s)." However, a more all-encompassing term such as "God-consciousness" or "God-mindfulness" will cover all these impersonal virtues.

Islamic ideas, particularly Taqwa and resilience, work together to strengthen mental health and resilience. By exploring this fascinating relationship, we extend a warm invitation to comprehend and accept Islam's profound wisdom. Taqwa promotes behaviours and ideas consistent with morality and faith, emphasising a person's knowledge of God in all facets of life.

> *Allah (SWT) states: "And whoever is mindful of Allah, He will make a way out for them, and provide for them from sources they could never imagine. And whoever puts their trust in Allah, then He 'alone' is sufficient for them. Certainly, Allah achieves His Will. Allah has already set a destiny for everything." (Quran 65:2-3)*

These verses remind us that we're guaranteed Allah's (SWT) protection when we have Tawakkul, faith in Him, and Taqwa, awareness of Him. However, what does it mean to be cognisant of God and to keep this consciousness?

To put it simply, having Taqwa protects us from disobeying Allah (SWT) and remembering Him all the time. It involves continually reminding ourselves that Allah (SWT) is more significant than these issues and that we can manage them only so much. No matter how lost we may feel in life, if we maintain strong Taqwa and Tawakkul, Allah (SWT) will give us the direction we need to find the light to navigate both the highs and lows of life.

To become a mirror of lovely manifestations, the heart must be protected against everything that pulls a person away from Allah (SWT) or from anything other than Him. This is known as Taqwa. The act of Taqwa is when a believer runs to Allah's (SWT) safety and protection, carefully guards against things that may cause them suffering in the Hereafter, and separates themselves from sin to embrace good deeds.

The pinnacle of Taqwa is reached when the servant, to the extent that it is possible, directs their entire existence towards Allah (SWT) while shielding their heart from anything that could cause it to become careless. This final phase is the actual Taqwa that the verse below commands:

> *"O you who have attained to faith, Be conscious of Allah with all the consciousness that is due to Him and do not allow death to overtake you before you have surrendered yourselves unto Him." (Quran 3:102)*

The believer must always consider their soul to get Taqwa. This is because the only way to fortify one's Taqwa is to withstand the strong cravings of the evil-commanding soul, which is the heart's worst enemy, and shield it from its tricks.

Fundamentally, Taqwa is the compass that points a believer toward living a moral life. The inner power continuously reminds one of one's obligation to Allah (SWT) and supports one in making decisions that please Him. Taqwa can be the light that guides us through many obstacles and shows us the way to righteousness and everlasting success.

> *As Allah (SWT) states in the Quran: "Verily, in the remembrance of Allah do hearts find rest." (Quran 13:28)*

Peace and calmness fill the heart as one considers and remembers the magnificence of Allah (SWT). Finding solace in Him during difficult times might help one feel at ease. The verse emphasises that having a close relationship with Allah (SWT) is the only way to find true consolation and inner peace.

It reminds us that while material pursuits and worldly diversions may provide momentary happiness, the only place to find true tranquillity is in remembering our Creator. Even in the face of life's obstacles and hardships, we can develop a condition of awareness, thankfulness, and serenity by routinely participating in acts of memory.

"The best of provision is Taqwa (God-consciousness)."
(Quran 2:197)

God-consciousness leads a person to be righteous, God-fearing, self-restraining, and self-refraining from sinful act(s). Hence, that is the spiritual taqwa that protects oneself from all harm that comes his way, both physically and spiritually.

Fostering a close relationship with Allah through regular acts of worship

Fostering a close relationship with Allah (SWT) through regular acts of worship is central to nurturing both spiritual and mental well-being. This relationship provides a sense of peace, purpose, and resilience, helping to navigate life's challenges with a calm and centred mind. Let's have a look at the acts of worship through which a believer can cultivate a profound sense of closeness to Allah (SWT), experiencing His mercy, guidance, and protection in all aspects of life.

- **Shahada (Faith)**

The Shahada, the Islamic declaration of faith, is the foundation of a Muslim's belief and a direct connection to Allah (SWT). The core of Islam is the conviction that "There is no god but Allah (SWT), and Muhammad (PBUH) is the Messenger of Allah (SWT)."

This Arabic phrase appears prominently featured in various works of architecture and artefacts, such as the Quran, the sacred book of Islam that contains revelations from Allah (SWT). Reciting this Shahada with sincere belief is a sign of being a true Muslim. It is the most revered verse in Islam and should be recited with complete comprehension and awareness of its significance.

The Shahada is a declaration of faith that also represents a promise to live an Islamically guided-life. It is recited at several daily prayers, the Adhan (call to prayer), and significant events like the conversion to Islam.

In addition to serving as a testament to Islamic beliefs, the Shahada serves as a common bond for Muslims from all backgrounds and cultures. It serves as the cornerstone of the common beliefs and principles that Muslims uphold, highlighting the significance of devotedly adhering to Allah's (SWT) will and His last messenger, Muhammad (PBUH).

There is only one god but Allah (SWT): This passage in the Shahada restates the monotheistic conviction in Allah's (SWT) unicity. It declares that Allah (SWT), the one and only God, is the only deity or god deserving of worship. This proclamation is the core of Islamic monotheism.

Muhammad PBUH is Allah's (SWT) Messenger: The Shahada's second section recognises Muhammad's (PBUH) prophetic status. Muslims consider Muhammad (PBUH) to be the last prophet sent by Allah (SWT) to guide humanity. Muslims who acknowledge him as the final messenger pledge to abide by his precepts and the Quran, the sacred text revealed to him.

Reciting the Shahada encourages mindfulness and awareness of Allah's (SWT) presence in daily life. It serves as a spiritual anchor, reminding Muslims to live according to the principles of Islam and to seek Allah's (SWT) guidance in all matters. This heightened awareness fosters a deeper, more conscious connection to Allah (SWT).

- **Prayer (Salah)**

The second most significant pillar of Islam after the Shahada is the Salah, a unique form of devotion. This type of prayer was taught to us by the Holy Prophet (PBUH) and revealed in the Holy Quran. This desired success calls to us five times a day.

The Prophet (PBUH) said: "The first thing which will be judged among a person's deed on the Day of Resurrection is the Prayer (Salah). If this is in good order, he will succeed and prosper, but if it is defective, he will fail and lose." (Tirmidhi)

Allah (SWT) emphasises the value of prayer in numerous verses throughout the Holy Quran.

"But those who hold fast to the Book and establish prayer – Indeed We will not allow to be lost the reward of the pious." (Quran 7:170)

"Recite, [O Muhammad], what has been revealed to you of the Book and establish prayer. Indeed, prayer prohibits immorality and wrongdoing, and the remembrance of Allah is greater. And Allah knows that which you do." (Quran 29:45)

Salah involves several bodily actions, including standing, bowing down, prostrating, and sitting. Along with several dua, it also entails reading Arabic passages from the Holy Quran (supplications). Every time we pray, we should face the Kabah, the Sacred House of Allah (SWT) in Makkah. The purpose of these gestures, incantations, and bodily motions is to demonstrate humility and surrender to Allah (SWT).

Muslims pray because they believe that worshipping Allah (SWT) alone is the ultimate goal of life. One of the first commands that Allah (SWT) gave to Prophet Muhammad (PBUH) when he became a prophet was to do Salah (worship).

"And I (Allah SWT) created not the jinn and humans except they should worship Me (Alone)."(Quran 51:56)

So, this second pillar of Islam, Salah, is essential to a Muslim's faith. It is the main distinction between Muslims and non-Muslims. The Prophet (PBUH) said:

"Between a man and polytheism and disbelief, there stands his neglect of the prayer." (Sahih Muslim)

Whether ritualistic or not, worshipping Allah (SWT) as he is portrayed in Islam purifies life by discouraging evil thoughts and deeds. In fact, a person who practices true Islamic worship is trained to live a life of total surrender to Allah (SWT).

A believer's relationship with Allah (SWT) is a crucial component of their religion, and there is no better way to demonstrate this relationship than via prayer. When someone prays with passion and sincerity, their heart will be filled with the love of Allah (SWT) and the hope of Paradise, lifting them spiritually towards their Creator. Muslims can better recall Allah (SWT) and ask for His pardon and pleasure by praying five times a day. Additionally, it provides a chance for repentance, whereby they humbly beg Allah's (SWT) pardon for the transgressions they committed.

Prophet Muhammad (PBUH) said: "Imagine a stream outside a person's door and imagine that he bathes in it five times a day; do you think he would have any dirt on him?" The people said, "Not at all." The Prophet (PBUH) then said, "The five daily prayers are like that: Allah (SWT) wipes away the sins by them." (Sahih Bukhari)

The fundamental element of an individual's connection with the divine is their fervent belief and genuineness. Prayer amplifies and confirms this relationship with Allah (SWT). An individual will be changed permanently if the prayer is said with genuine devotion to Allah (SWT) and an honest heart. Therefore, prayer helps Muslims communicate regularly with their Creator and maintain composure in the face of life's pressures and temptations.

- **Quran Recitation**

Muslims use the Quran as material and spiritual guidance. The Quran's lessons apply to everyone. They illuminate the route to the afterlife and the spirit of man. Islam highly values the Quran because it provides a comprehensive framework for morality, behaviour, and belief. Prophet Muhammad (PBUH) lived a life that embodied the teachings of the Quran, highlighting the book's crucial significance in forming Muslims' moral principles. Believers achieve spiritual fulfilment and comfort by drawing inspiration and guidance from the Quran daily.

Allah (SWT) clearly stated: "This is a blessed Book We have revealed. So follow it and be mindful ˹of Allah˺, so you may be shown mercy." (Quran 7:96)

He also stated: "There certainly has come to you from Allah a light and a clear Book through which Allah guides those who seek His pleasure to the ways of peace, brings them out of darkness and into light by His Will, and guides them to the Straight Path." (Quran 5:15)

Frequent prayer and Quran recitation remind us of our life's purpose and the ideals and standards we ought to pursue. Through these acts of worship, we can speak with Allah (SWT) and ask for His blessings and guidance. Quranic recitation enhances this connection. The Quran is believed to be Allah's (SWT) direct word to humanity, and reading it closely strengthens that bond.

• Dua and Dhikr (Remembrance)

One of the most exquisite Islamic rituals is dua. Muslims can use dua to communicate with Allah (SWT), serving as the most effective means of supplication, communication, and invocation. For believers, dua is a vital aspect of their faith since it builds a bridge between the servant and the Lord and also fosters a deeper connection with oneself.

Prophet Muhammad (PBUH) said: "The most excellent worship is Dua." (Sahih Al-Jami)

As dua is an exchange between Muslims and the Almighty Allah (SWT), it is the greatest kind of mediation and offers hope and mental serenity. Although we cannot see or touch Allah (SWT), we can nevertheless sense Him through performing good deeds and participating in religious rituals.

Allah (SWT) is always listening to us, so talk to Him about everything on your mind. He also sees you at all times, so do good deeds. Finally, Allah (SWT) is waiting for you to repent of any intentional or inadvertent sins you've committed. Finally, He is willing to grant you everything you could ever want, so please call Him.

Allah (SWT) has repeatedly stated in the Quran that He is always with us and that we should call on Him at any time, no matter what. Muslims are encouraged to remember their Creator and follow His guidance to maintain in constant communication with Him.

Dua can be performed at any time; it is not required to do so after Iftar (following a fast) or after Salah. Islam is the simplest religion because it offers straightforward ways to deepen one's relationship with Allah (SWT).

"Verily in the remembrance of Allah do hearts find rest."
(Quran 13:28)

In a similar vein, Dhikr is an outward and interior manifestation of Allah (SWT)'s memory. Dhikr is a silent prayer, done in the heart and mind, directed only towards Allah (SWT), no matter when or where it occurs. Dhikr goes beyond simple contemplation and can also be conveyed in recitations and supplications from the heart in memory of Allah (SWT). It is imperative to underscore the great relevance of this active type of Dhikr, particularly in the modern world.

In the modern world, distractions are plentiful and can quickly divert attention from what truly matters. Engaging in vocal or active versions of Dhikr is very useful for blocking out these distractions and keeping your attention on the purpose of remembering. Those with reason and insight, according to Allah (SWT), constantly remember Allah (SWT) in all facets of their existence.

"(They are) those who remember Allah while stand-ing, sitting, and lying on their sides, and reflect on the creation of the heavens and the earth (and pray), 'Our Lord! You have not created (all of) this without purpose. Glory be to You! Protect us from the torment of the Fire.'"
(Quran 3:191)

Regularly practising Dhikr demands dedication and practice, like any other excellent habit. Start small and practise the basic Dhikr of Allahu Akbar (Allah SWT is Great), La ilaha illallah (there is no real god but Allah SWT), SubhanAllah (Glory be to Allah SWT), and Alhamdulillah (Praise be to Allah SWT). The benefits of these excellent deeds outlast worldly joys; another name for this Dhikr: the everlasting good deeds.

The Prophet (PBUH) stated in a hadith that he loves to recite this particular Dhikr on a regular basis: "(The uttering of) 'SubhanAllah (Glory be to Allah), Alhamdulillah (Praise be to Allah), La ilaha illallah (there is no true god except Allah), and Allahu Akbar (Allah is Great)' is dearer to me than anything over which the sun rises." (Sahih Muslim)

Fostering a close relationship with Allah (SWT) through regular acts of worship is a lifelong journey that enriches both the spiritual and mental aspects of a believer's life. The practices of Shahada, Salah, Quran recitation, Dua, and Dhikr each play a crucial role in strengthening this divine connection.

Tawakkul (Reliance on Allah) is a Pillar of Resilience

Tawakkul, or reliance on Allah (SWT), is a central concept in Islam that signifies placing complete trust in Allah's (SWT) plan and wisdom. Tawakkul itself means "trust and reliance," which implies that it is somewhat dualistic and has two distinct aspects that are interconnected rather than independent.

The first Ayah that comes to mind when we think about Tawakkul (or confidence and reliance in Allah SWT) is:

"And He will provide him from sources he could never imagine. And whoever puts their trust in Allah (SWT), and then He will suffice him. Verily, Allah (SWT) will accomplish His purpose. Indeed, Allah (SWT) has set a measure for all things." (Quran 65:3)

Fundamentally, Tawakkul in the Islamic teachings signifies the act of putting all of one's reliance on Allah (SWT) and acknowledging His wisdom and omnipotence in the course of events, independent of human attempts. Although this could imply a passive faith in fate, Islam offers a sophisticated interpretation that combines human endeavour with Divine will.

> *The Quran highlights the significance of Tawakkul as: "[He is] the Lord of the East and the West; there is no deity except Him, so take Him as Disposer of [your] affairs.]"(Quran 73:9)*

The line captures the core of Tawakkul. It acknowledges the extent of God's dominion and our entrusting Him with our concerns in light of the fact that He is the only one in control of everything that exists in the East and the West. This unshakeable faith recognises that while we each play a part, Allah (SWT) ultimately determines the outcome, placing our effort within an almighty context rather than negating it.

Tawakkul strengthens resilience by offering inner peace and contentment, knowing Allah's (SWT) plan is always the best. This reliance on Allah (SWT) alleviates the anxiety of uncertainty, empowering believers to face adversity confidently.

Developing reliance on Allah's provisions (Rizq) and blessings (Barakah)

Muslims are aware of the importance of Rizq, or supply or nourishment, in daily life. This idea closely relates to our faith and represents Allah's (SWT) provisions for His creation. It is crucial that we coordinate our efforts with the Quran's teachings to find Rizq-e-halal. Rizq-e-halal is the Arabic term for a sincere and righteous living.

*Prophet (PBUH) said: "A soul will not die until it gets
all of the provision that has been apportioned for it."
(Musnad Ahmad)*

We must never forget that Allah (SWT) is the source of our nourishment. He alone has the ability to bestow upon us abundance, and no one can prevent Him from doing so if that is His desire. However, to do that, we must say Alhamdulillah for everything in our lives, abstain from major sins, donate as much as we can, pray on time, and set aside time to worship Allah (SWT). By carrying out these actions, we can earn and grow our Rizq (Provision) in a Halal manner.

*Allah (SWT) says in the Holy Quran: "And whosoever
puts his trust in Allah, then He will suffice him. Verily,
Allah will accomplish his purpose. Indeed Allah has set
a measure for all things." (At-Talaq, 65:3)*

Being firmly convinced that everything that happens to us and comes to us, whether it is provisions or other circumstances, is from Allah (SWT) is the genuine meaning of sincerely trusting Allah (SWT). Moreover, Tawakkul signifies exerting genuine effort and entrusting the outcome to Allah (SWT), depending on Him to ease our burdens and resolve issues.

A believer who is able to have this level of faith in Allah (SWT) is assured that He will provide a way out of any situation, including difficult financial circumstances.

Hence, Allah (SWT) promises that all living things will have plenty to eat. Sustenance includes things like health, work, position, and the chance to pray, in addition to having a family with a devout wife and kids.

Allah (SWT) said: "There is no moving creature on earth whose provision is not guaranteed by Allah. And He knows where it lives and where it is laid to rest. All is 'written' in a perfect Record..." (Quran 11:6)

At the same time, Barakah (blessings) is the divine increase or spiritual abundance of one's possessions. While Rizq is about what we receive, Barakah ensures that what we have is sufficient, beneficial, and fulfilling. Growth and increase are referred to as Barakah, and certain of Allah's slaves experience this blessing.

Our Prophet Muhammad (PBUH) offered prayers for Barakah for several people and events, including Anas ibn Malik (RA).

Prophet Muhammad (PBUH) prayed, "O Allah, increase his wealth and offspring, and bless what you have given him" (Bukhari)

After the Prophet (PBUH) asked Allah (SWT) to grant his requests, Hazrat Anas (RA) became one of the wealthiest Ansar and was bestowed with abundance, over a hundred children and grandchildren, and granted the blessing of living for more than a century.

Barakah is widely understood as a gift from Allah (SWT), who is the source of all Barakah and the supplier of all good things. Barakah can manifest at any time in a person's life, amplifying even the tiniest benefits and considerably increasing the larger ones. The ultimate aim of Barakah is to use these blessings in devotion to Allah (SWT), such as devoting money or time to acts of worship.

We ought to appreciate all the blessings Allah (SWT) has given us and be thankful for all He has given us. We far too frequently take our blessings for granted and fail to consider the various treasures we have been bestowed with. We are also reminded that our blessings will multiply if we express thanks.

> *"And [remember], when your Lord proclaimed, 'If you are grateful, I will surely increase you [in favour]; but if you show ingratitude, indeed, My Punishment is sever e.'" (Quran 14:7)*

Remember, life's challenges will never go away, but by adopting a different perspective, we can concentrate on the countless benefits that far outweigh the difficulties. Allah (SWT) will enhance us in good and bless us if we demonstrate contentment in what has been determined.

Developing reliance on Allah's (SWT) provisions and blessings is a journey of the heart and soul. It involves trusting in His wisdom, seeking halal means of Rizq, expressing gratitude, and remaining content with His decree. By embracing Tawakkul, practising Shukr, and making sincere Dua, we invite Barakah into our lives, ensuring that our Rizq is sufficient and blessed.

Overcoming anxiety and fear through trust in Allah's plan

Throughout our lives, we frequently work towards realising our goals and desires. We believe we know what is best for us; therefore, we carefully plan and strive towards our goals. But it is vital for us as believers to recognise that Allah's (SWT) plan is greater than our finite perception and comprehension. The idea of submitting to His heavenly direction serves as a sobering reminder that the great plan He has for us may surpass our wildest expectations.

When we encounter difficulties, disappointments, or unforeseen changes, we often get discouraged and wonder what direction we are headed. It is vital to remember that Allah (SWT), the Most Wise, knows what is best for His creation at such times. He sees past our current situation and knows all the nuances in our lives.

How often have you felt frustrated that things seemed to be falling apart, only to look back months or years later and see that everything came together like a carefully thought-out plan? How often do you find reflecting on past events helps you understand why things ultimately worked out for the best?

Allah states in the Quran: "And Allah is the best of planners." (Quran 8:30)

"But perhaps you hate a thing and it is good for you; and perhaps you love a thing and it is bad for you. And Allah knows, while you know not" (Quran 2:216)

Sometimes, understanding comes with time, but other times, not even years later, it may remain unclear why certain events happened for the better. In times such as these, it is helpful to recall the suffering and tribulations endured by the Prophets and righteous individuals of the past and how seemingly unfavourable circumstances worked out for the best. Such tales abound throughout the Quran.

Hazrat Musa's (AS) mother was instructed to cast her infant into the river; Hazrat Yaqub (AS) spent years apart from his son Hazrat Yusuf (AS); Hazrat Maryam (AS) gave birth to a baby by herself and was afraid of being accused by those in her immediate vicinity. All of these situations worked out for the best.

Even though Hazrat Musa (AS) was raised in the Pharaoh's (Islam's worst enemy) court, his mother gave him back to prepare him for his upcoming job. For Hazrat Yusuf (AS) to arrive at the positions he eventually attained, his brothers had to abandon him in the well. And

Hazrat Maryam (AS) was protected by her young son and honoured throughout history.

When we trust Allah (SWT), we urge ourselves to keep going even when it's difficult on the route He has for us. When we trust Allah (SWT), we do not doubt His will—even when we are overcome with fears. When we trust Allah (SWT), we put our trust in Him to guide us through this, to put us on the exact route we are supposed to be on and to eventually show us why this was all for the best.

Through the idea of divine decision and destiny, Allah's (SWT) purpose is revealed. We are taught that everything in our lives—good or bad—has a purpose and is part of a bigger scheme. Occasionally, this plan may not match our aspirations and desires, leaving us disappointed or perplexed.

But during these times, we must acknowledge that Allah's (SWT) purpose is much bigger than our comprehension. He directs the course of events in our lives to mould us, hone our personalities, and eventually point us toward what is best for us.

In trusting Allah's (SWT) plan, we find peace and resilience, knowing that every event unfolds with divine wisdom beyond our understanding. By surrendering to His guidance, we overcome fear and anxiety, confident that all will work out for our ultimate good.

Chapter Five

Patience and Perseverance (Sabr)

Virtues and Benefits of Sabr in Islam

Although patience is the typical understanding of Sabr, it encompasses more. When we exercise restraint in a challenging circumstance, we demonstrate patience. However, the concept of Sabr also includes perseverance. The heart needs both tenacity and patience to get what it wants.

In Islam, Muslims are required by Allah (SWT) to exhibit great endurance and tenacity on a regular basis. As Allah (SWT) promised, our efforts and hardships, when paired with the fear of Allah (SWT), will result in success in this world and the next:

"O you who have believed, persevere and endure and remain stationed and fear Allah that you may be successful." (Quran 3:200)

Allah (SWT) commands us to bear with patience and endurance whatsoever adversities we encounter. If Allah (SWT) so desires, we will have days of ease and days of trouble. Furthermore, we don't always get our wishes fulfilled. In any circumstance, we ought to exercise patience.

Even though it is well known that we will always face tests in this life, we will occasionally find that we forget. We, therefore, wonder when we are being challenged because of this forgetfulness. Adversity can be a test from Allah (SWT); thus, those who recognise this will handle it patiently in the hopes of receiving a reward from their lord.

Allah (SWT) puts us to the test. In trying times, a sincere believer will wait for help, be patient, and think well of his Lord. Some people go quickly for solace somewhere other than Allah (SWT), while others believe they are suffering unfairly and that they have no business being in such circumstances. This is not how sincere believers think or approach things.

Rather, they turn back to their Allah (SWT) and ask for His pardon and assistance, then wait for solace. Some people can also be placed in difficult situations to make amends for their transgressions, turn away from their sins, and seek Allah's (SWT) pleasure.

In Islamic tradition, the Prophet Muhammad (PBUH) is regarded as a model of patience. There are several examples throughout his life of exhibiting incredible patience in the face of severe adversity.

The significant influence that Sabr (patience) has on a person's well-being, spiritual development, and ability to withstand adversity is highlighted in Islamic psychology. Quranic passages and the teachings of Prophet Muhammad (PBUH) are the foundation of its significance.

Throughout his 13 years as a prophet in Makkah, the Prophet Muhammad (PBUH) exhibited patience. He endured great suffering and persecution but never wavered in his resolve or patience.

Being patient in the midst of hardship is seen as a sign of emotional resilience. Emotional stability and the capacity to face obstacles in life without giving in to unpleasant feelings are both facilitated by practising patience.

The relationship between spiritual elevation and patience is emphasised throughout the Quran. According to Surah Al-Baqarah (2:155–157), blessings and a closer relationship with Allah (SWT) are guaranteed to those who patiently face hardships. This link between spiritual growth and patience emphasises the centrality of patience in the Islamic psychological system.

In Islamic psychology, sabr is significant because it is a transformational force that promotes not only spiritual development but also emotional fortitude, constructive coping, self-control, and healing. These psychological aspects are woven within Islam's holistic philosophy, assisting followers in developing robust and balanced minds. Let's find how it can positively impact our lives.

We understand that the patient, also known as the Sabirun, will receive great rewards in the Hereafter for their endurance and perseverance through life's trials. Yet, the practice of Sabr can greatly assist us in our daily lives and spiritual journey, even when significant hardships are rare and far between.

Let's use an illustration. Suppose someone finds it difficult to read the Quran. He wants to stop reciting and limit Arabic reading to special occasions because he finds it so difficult to read. This difficulty has left him feeling quite discouraged. Why, after all, go to all this trouble when he does not even understand what he's reading? Would it not be preferable to simply read the meaning as translated? Is there any way he can gain more from it?

He is aware that the response is "no." Yes, comprehension is required, but it's also essential to recite the text in its original Arabic. Thus, he resists the urges and decides to support Sabr in this conflict. He is also aware that one of Islam's most crucial teachings is gradualism:

"The deeds most loved by Allah (are those) done regular-ly, even if they are small." (Bukhari and Muslim)

Therefore, he perseveres patiently and chooses to read just two verses a day. Allah (SWT) thinks highly of this modest, controlled, and regular effort, and as time passes and He finds recitation becoming easier and easier, He raises his daily allotment. Thus, this modest beginning blossomed into significant outcomes, allowing him to be increasingly fruitful in his spiritual life.

The application of Sabr as Muslims can be made to any aspect of our faith, including acquiring knowledge that can benefit you, developing your character, and increasing the depth of your faith and Taqwa. Patience promotes a calm and reasoned response to adversity rather than an impetuous one.

Sabr for productivity in Dunya (this life)

Think about your career or academic pursuits. Let's say you have a large assignment due and detest your work immensely. Maybe you think the task is too hard, the topic isn't engaging enough, or you're just doing it to support someone, even though you don't want to.

A lot of us will start, but the real problems come when we encounter the first roadblock. Our brains constantly provide us with reasons to "take a break" from our tasks. We'll put off doing the assignment until the last minute because we'll find other things to do that are "more important."

Even the best among us are prone to procrastination, but bearing Sabr is a guaranteed method to overcome the habit. When you are sacrificial in your work, especially when it's work you detest, you become more productive. This approach encourages you to push yourself to finish the task rather than putting it off. By breaking the work into manageable chunks and finding ways to make it more enjoyable, you enhance your ability to finish the assignment. By doing this, you also challenge yourself to go beyond mental boundaries.

Applying Sabr can increase your productivity not only at work but in many other 'worldly' areas of life as well, such as administrative work, cleaning and organising your room or house, mending damaged items, organising your cabinets, and much more.

In sum, Sabr is not just a passive act of waiting but an active engagement in maintaining faith, trust, and reliance on Allah (SWT) during life's challenges. It is a powerful tool that shapes a believer's character, purifies the soul, and strengthens the connection with Allah (SWT), ultimately leading to success in this life and the Hereafter.

Understanding the different types of patience (Sabr) and their rewards

We are taught as Muslims that there are three main categories of Sabr.

- Sabr in following Allah's (SWT) instructions.

- Sabr in refraining from Allah's (SWT) prohibitions.

- Sabr in accepting Allah's (SWT) plan when disaster strikes.

The first type of patience involves being steadfast in obedience to Allah(SWT). Obedience weighs heavily on the spirit, has certain challenging features, and can be physically taxing to the point where a person feels exhausted and unable. Even when performing Hajj or paying Zakah, a person may face financial difficulties.

Moreover, performing acts of worship (Ibadah) requires patience. It takes time, strength, and energy to carry out acts like Salah, fasting, and required charity, in addition to faith. If a person is impatient or lazy when performing their Ibadah, it may not be completed properly or with the required sincerity.

The second kind of Sabr involves exercising patience to abstain from the prohibitions. A person's soul drives them towards evil, so they must exercise patience in resisting their soul by abstaining from forbidden behaviours in Islam.

Therefore, to avoid committing evil deeds, a person must exercise self-control, which requires endurance and tolerance. It takes a lot of willpower to resist one's cravings and patience to avoid Shaytan's (devil) wicked influences and abstain from forbidden deeds.

Things that are forbidden can occasionally pique our interest, and resisting them demands strong willpower and determination, especially when we desire them. The willpower and fortitude required to refrain from sins are a type of patience, as one understands that by resisting immediate temptations, one will reap greater benefits later.

> *"So be patient for the decision of your Lord and do not obey from among them a sinner or ungrateful [disbeliever]." (Quran 76:24)*

The final type of patience is demonstrated by someone who remains calm in the face of adversity and doesn't complain. There is nothing to be upset over because Allah (SWT) has already planned life's tribulations.

The believers will remain calm and say "Alhamdulillah" for the chance to become closer to Allah (SWT), viewing hardship as a chance to adore Him. Since Allah (SWT) is the one who created everything, it doesn't matter what we lose in the end because we must all return to Him.

When faced with misfortunes and disasters, we have been instructed to exercise patience—even more so when it initially happens. Knowing that every misfortune is an exam from Allah (SWT) helps one to be more patient.

"You will surely be tested in your possessions and in yourselves. And you will surely hear from those who were given the Scripture before you and from those who associate others with Allah much abuse. But if you are patient and fear Allah – indeed, that is of the matters [worthy] of determination." (Quran 3:186)

Practising patience in trials and hardships with unwavering faith

Everybody faces different levels of hardship and obstacles in their lives. However, protracted misfortunes or tribulations like severe or chronic disease, conflict with family members, and financial difficulties start to wear down our faith and connection with Allah (SWT), putting our fortitude and faith to the test.

Long-term adversity wears you out and requires patience, which can be hard to practise, but it is so rewarding. If a person waits long enough to experience adversity, they may question whether Allah (SWT) loves them or is even aware of their duas (supplications). However, if a person's struggle is brief, they could see the result of their duas sooner, leaving less space for uncertainty.

Generally speaking, people assume that if they experience extreme suffering like hunger, terror, or loss, it indicates that they are cursed rather than rewarded. However, Allah (SWT) clarifies that these folks are being led correctly and are receiving benefits and mercy from their Lord.

This demonstrates that facing hardships does not imply that one has lost Allah Almighty's favour or that He no longer loves them; rather, it allows one to demonstrate patience and the strength of one's faith. This does not imply that we should wish for misfortune or rejoice when it does.

Thus, in times of hardship, pray to Allah (SWT) for ease, trusting in His wisdom and mercy. Patience in adversity not only strengthens your faith but brings you closer to Allah (SWT), knowing that every trial is an opportunity for growth and reward.

Techniques for Cultivating Patience and Endurance

In a world driven by instant gratification, it's easy to lose patience. It's simple to become angry, irritated, and eventually depressed when things don't go our way. It's difficult to be collected and peaceful when we're constantly surrounded by demands, expectations, and diversions. But as Muslims, we must be aware of the importance of patience as a virtue that is fundamental to our religion. Let's have a look at useful advice on developing this crucial trait.

Adopting a positive mindset (Husn al-Dhan) and reframing challenges as opportunities

Though its literal translation is "having good, positive thoughts," the meaning of Husn al-Dhan is much more profound. There are two facets of Husn al-Dhan in Islam.

With Allah (SWT):

Meaning of Husn al-Dhan Billah:

- To think positively about Allah (SWT) and

- To have the utmost faith in Him.

Having a positive expectation of Allah (SWT) is like creating a self-fulfilling prophecy – what you expect is what you receive. To fully rely on Allah (SWT), you ought to have high expectations for Him.

In essence, Husn al-Dhan Billah means being certain that Allah (SWT) loves you because He made you, cares for you, heals you, and hears you until the point of death, at which point He will take you back.

The ideal source of a person's sense of safety, love, and connection should be Allah (SWT). It's the most wholesome variety. It makes one a better giver and seeker of love for others, and it strengthens all other relationships.

> *"And when you have decided, then rely upon Allah. Indeed, Allah loves those who rely [upon Him]." (Quran 3:159)*

Most Muslims overlook the fact that love or a genuine desire to seek love is the cornerstone upon which an essential link between a human and Allah (SWT) is based. When you approach Islam from this angle, it can drastically change not just how you worship but also how you express the compassionate nature of this faith to others.

With People:

In human interactions, Husn al-Dhan refers to giving others the benefit of the doubt. It's a proactive mindset where we actively look for and give good explanations for other people's conduct rather than merely trying to find excuses for them. The less you assume the worst about other people, the more likely they will trust you. Everyone dislikes being judged just as much as we do.

According to the Prophet (PBUH), thinking well of other people is a lovely kind of worship. Therefore, we should intentionally work to cultivate a good outlook and consciously execute and perfect our worship.

If you don't practise Husn al-Dhan with others and instead default to drawing unfavourable judgements about them, you ultimately do more harm to yourself than to anyone else. This mindset disturbs your own peace of mind. By avoiding negative thoughts about others, you'll find that your personal inner peace and the calibre of your relationships improve.

Adopting positivity and cultivating a positive mindset is a powerful practice that encourages Muslims to remain optimistic when facing hardships or difficulties. Each difficulty carries within it the seeds of potential transformation.

By shifting our mindset, we open ourselves to discovering new solutions, developing skills, and strengthening our character. This approach not only helps in overcoming adversity but also enriches our lives by revealing the hidden blessings in every situation.

By embracing Husn al-Dhan, we trust in this divine wisdom and allow it to guide us through life's trials, turning them into opportunities for success and fulfilment.

Chapter Six

Seeking Guidance through Salah (Prayer)

Role of Salah in Seeking Guidance and Support

Have you ever wondered why Salah is important in Islam? What effect does it have on the lives of Muslims globally?

Salah's significance in Islam is that first it is one of the five pillars of Islam, and practising it consistently has several advantages. It is a direct channel for Muslims to approach Allah (SWT) to ask for mercy and guidance.

Salah not only fortifies faith but also instils discipline in day-to-day living, encouraging accountability and dedication. It provides health benefits as well, including stress reduction and increased flexibility. All things considered, Salah is essential to a Muslim's bodily and spiritual health.

In the current world, almost everyone engages in some form of daily life activities, such as working, attending school or the office, consuming food, sleeping, and interacting with others. Of course, due to our busy and hectic lives, we often neglect our duties towards Allah (SWT). This life and its concerns take up most of a person's mental activity when they ignore Allah (SWT). Wants are unbridled. Someone starts to "chase his shadow," which is unachievable.

That's why certain periods of the day are necessary for Muslims to regularly take a short break from their daily routines to spend time with Allah (SWT). This time can be initially when we wake up, during the day (in the middle of the afternoon), in the evening after work, or at night before sleep. When carried out correctly and with focus, it awakens and stimulates the soul.

A Muslim constantly reminds himself that Allah (SWT) is sovereign over all things, that he is Allah's (SWT) obedient servant, and that Allah's (SWT) pleasure is his ultimate goal. Five times a day, for a short while, a Muslim transcends this world to meet His Lord:

> *Allah (SWT) says: "And establish the prayers (Salah) in order to remember Me." (Quran 20:14)*

Salah is more than just a regular practice; it's a powerful chance to deepen one's relationship with Allah (SWT) and ask for forgiveness. Let's investigate all its aspects!

Five daily prayers

Salah is more than just a once-a-week or sporadic act of prayer in Islam. Muslims have this duty, which they must perform five times a day at certain times. These are the following:

- Fajr: this occurs just before dawn.

- Dhuhr: this occurs immediately following the sun's zenith.

- Asr: this happens from midday till dusk.

- Maghrib: this occurs shortly after dusk.

- Isha: this happens at night or during the night.

These hadith help us understand the significance of praying salah on time:

Abdullah (RA) asked the Prophet Muhammad (PBUH), "Which deed is the dearest to Allah?" He replied, "To offer the prayers at their early stated fixed times." (Sahih Bukhari)

As narrated by Ibn Umar, Prophet (PBUH) said: "The beginning of the time for Salah is pleasing to Allah (SWT), and the end of its time is pardoned by Allah (SWT)." (Tirmidhi)

Therefore, to satisfy Allah (SWT), who is necessary for you to be granted a position in Jannah, don't you wish to start the prayer as soon as possible?

Since we are weak by nature, we can quickly stray from righteousness if we don't seek guidance from Allah (SWT). Therefore, wouldn't it be desirable for you to ask Allah (SWT) for assistance in avoiding harm?

If you pray on time and early enough, Allah (SWT) will lead you and stop you from sinning.

As Muslims, we must always perform good deeds and be ready for our Akhirah. Our souls depart from our bodies anytime, and life continues eternally after death. As a result, we ought to offer Salah on time and make every effort to offer Salah early in the day.

Establishing regular prayers as a source of spiritual connection and guidance

Muslims must prepare both physically and psychologically for Salah, a spiritual and physical practice. It is necessary to ensure one is ritually pure before offering Salah by doing an ablution (Wudu). This purification process indicates that the body and soul are ready for a private discussion with Allah (SWT).

Salah's bodily positions, which include sitting (Sujood), standing (Qiyam), bowing (Ruku), and prostrating (Sujud), represent acts of humility and surrender. They act as a reminder that when one is in Allah's (SWT) presence, they should bend down in submission and ask for His forgiveness and guidance.

Muslims can develop virtues like humility and modesty, achieve inner peace, and enhance their faith through consistent prayer. Although the main source of spiritual enlightenment for believers is said to be the soul-illuminating benefits of prayer, prayer is also acknowledged for its ability to purify mankind as a whole.

The best way to exercise self-control, rein in our wild cravings, and stop a rebellious spirit is to keep Allah (SWT) in mind. When someone prays, they are always in the awareness of Allah (SWT), the Almighty, who is fully aware of all of their deepest thoughts and feelings as well as acutely aware of all of their major and tiny transgressions. The smallest result of remembering Allah (SWT) is that it balances one's ego and desires.

Additionally, prayers (Salah) increase awareness of the Almighty. A person who prays five times a day becomes used to sensing God's presence and starts believing that Allah (SWT) is always keeping an eye on them. Even when they are alone, they are never truly hidden from Allah (SWT).

This consciousness of God maintains the heart halfway between hope and terror. A Muslim's fear of Allah (SWT) is a combination of heavenly love and fervent adoration, ensuring that they remain spiritually attentive. It helps them avoid forbidden things and motivates them to fulfil their obligations. Praying on a regular basis raises one's awareness of Allah (SWT).

We must continually seek Allah's (SWT) pardon and try to learn from our mistakes. Without regular communication with Allah (SWT), a person is unlikely to experience regret for their sins and turn from them. Over time, if one neglects to ask for Allah's (SWT) forgiveness, they may lose awareness of their sins and may even forget having committed them. As a result, they may stop seeking pardon altogether.

A few formal prayers (Salah) prompt Muslims to reflect on their transgressions and ask for forgiveness. Muslims consequently become repentant of their faults as soon as they commit them and feel bad about them. Through regular prayer, a Muslim learns to stay connected with their loving Lord, asking for forgiveness frequently. Prayer allows a person to approach Allah (SWT) directly and ask for forgiveness for their transgressions.

Moreover, prayer has the power to transform lives for the better. The discipline required to pause what we are doing and line up behind a prayer leader (Imam) five times a day in the mosque or find a private space to pray, whether at work or school, instils a sense of order and structure. Islam also permits flexibility in many situations, recognising that each person's circumstances are unique. For example, the Imam is encouraged to lead a brief prayer, women are not obligated to pray in the mosque, and a sick person can pray while seated or, in extreme cases, while lying down.

We should develop the discipline learned in prayer in various spheres of our religious and secular lives. Prayer teaches us to perform particular actions and say specific words at particular times. Every bodily part is subordinate to worshipping and following Allah (SWT); if this discipline is violated, the prayer might need to be repeated.

Just as we should not glance about while praying, we must also restrict our gaze from falling on any forbidden objects when we are not praying. Outside of our official prayers, we should avoid using our tongues to lie or backbite, and similarly, our hands or feet should not be used to steal, purchase, or consume anything banned outside of prayer. We should move away from the forbidden rather than towards it. This is the main thing that Allah (SWT) explains to us:

> *"...Surely, the prayer (Salah) prevents evil speech and bad deeds..." (Quran 29:45)*

In addition to this, the profound focus that leads to a sense of peace and tranquillity combined with humility is a crucial component of the prayer. In the Quran, Allah declares:

> *"Successful indeed are the believers, those who humble themselves in their prayers." (Quran 23:1-2)*

Prayer serves a purpose beyond merely performing a meaningless ritual. Prayer needs to be offered passionately to be accepted. Acquire knowledge of the definitions of Arabic words utilised in the prayer, paying particular attention to them and the passages of the Quran you will recite. Recognise that Allah (SWT) hears and answers your prayers. If something around you is distracting you and preventing you from focusing elsewhere, close your eyes and concentrate only on the area where you are prostrating.

One can improve their presence of mind during prayer by focusing on the words of the prayer as they are uttered in various postures, increasing awareness that they are in front of Allah (SWT), and selecting a quiet, distraction-free area. There's always going to be something better. Clear your mind and concentrate on Allah's (SWT) gifts in life, acknowledge your smallness in the eyes of the All-Powerful Creator, and feel sorry for your transgressions. You'll feel less stressed, anxious, and worried as a result.

Prayer is soul-healing, but to achieve this level of focus in your Salah, you must be patient and seek help from Allah (SWT) in all circumstances. In prayer, it takes consistent effort and struggle to attain a high degree of focus and humility. Recall! You are linked to your Creator through it.

Muslims who offer prayers daily develop a close relationship with Allah (SWT), which calms and peacefully occupies their hearts. In the end, regular prayers lead believers on a journey of spiritual development and fulfilment by acting as a continual reminder of the meaning of life and the significance of worship.

Finding clarity and solace through heartfelt conversations with Allah

For Muslims, conversations with Allah (SWT) are like opening your heart to Allah (SWT) and engaging in a sacred dialogue that transcends words. This practice clarifies life's challenges as you seek guidance and wisdom from the One who knows all.

In moments of gloom, bereavement, hardship, Ibtilaa (tests of faith), or extreme necessity, a wish may be amplified, leaving our hearts with a stronger desire than ever to communicate with Allah (SWT) directly. In Islam, it is advised that as soon as something needs to be said, just say it; let the prayer flow, say the dua right away, for you never know when it will be accepted. At any moment, whether you're strolling, driving, at home, or in the kitchen, call out to Allah (SWT), question Him, and share your thoughts with Him.

As the Creator, Almighty Allah (SWT) speaks with His creation. He uses a variety of methods, the majority of which remain undiscovered by humans. He tells us, for instance, that He speaks with fire, hellfire, animals, earth, mountains, skies, and so on through His revealed Word, the Holy Quran.

"It is not fitting for a man that Allah (SWT) should speak to him except by inspiration or from behind a veil or by the sending of a Messenger to reveal with Allah's permission what Allah wills, for He is Most High Most Wise." (Quran 42:51)

The Quran is the means by which Allah (SWT) speaks with us. He gives us instructions, warnings, directions, and an explanation of a significant transcendent truth. Examine the Quran with thoughtfulness, conviction, and purpose. Pay close attention to what Allah (SWT) says; he wants us to hear it all. The Quran is a manual for improving one's life and for practice, not theory. It actually has an answer to every question. Allah (SWT) sent it to us as a gift so that it would endure the test of time and provide answers to all of our questions. Accept that. Pay attention to what the Quran says. This is the way Allah (SWT) speaks to us.

Additionally, Salah offers a direct and intimate line of communication with Allah (SWT). Muslims are encouraged to use the Sujood (prostration), a period of extreme humility and submission, to supplicate, ask for pardon for their transgressions, voice their worries, and express gratitude. This intimate connection to Allah (SWT) offers an opportunity for self-reflection and spiritual growth. It provides consolation, inner calm, and a sensation of being heard, all strengthening a person's relationship with their Creator.

Special Prayer as a source of guidance

Muslims who are faced with important life decisions often pray Salah al-Istikhara, which refers to the Prayer of Seeking Counsel. This prayer is divided into two parts: Rakah and Salah al-Istikhara. It was discovered to be a legitimate replacement for belomancy, which is prohibited by Islam and was widespread in pre-Islamic Arabia. Just as the Holy Prophet (PBUH) used to teach his companions chapters from the Quran, He (PBUH) also taught them to seek the advice of Allah (SWT) in everything.

> *He said: "If any one of you is anxious about a decision pray two units Rakah of voluntary Salah prayer and say: "O Allah, I seek Your counsel through Your knowledge and I seek Your assistance through Your might and I ask You from Your immense favour, for verily You alone decree our fate while I do not, and You know while I do not, and You alone possess all knowledge of the Unseen. O Allah, if You know this matter (mention matter here) to be good for me in relation to my religion, my life and livelihood and the end of my affairs, my present and future, then decree it for me and facilitate it for me, and then place blessing for me within it, and if You know this affair to be harmful for me concerning my religion, my life and livelihood and the end of my affairs, then remove it from me and remove me from it, and decree for me what is good, wherever it may be, and make me content with it."' (Sahih Bukhari)*

Incorporating Dua (Supplication) into Daily Practices

Dua's, which are Islamic prayers and invocations to Allah (SWT), are called supplications. For Muslims, learning and applying dua daily is essential to worship and developing a relationship with Allah (SWT). Muslims are, therefore, urged to incorporate supplications for all areas of their lives, believing that Allah's (SWT) knowledge and compassion are universal.

Harnessing the power of sincere supplications during challenging times

You can ask Allah (SWT) for help through dua when you're having problems with your health, profession, relationships, or anything else in your life. In Arabic, "Dua" means "calling" or "summoning." Making a dua is essentially admitting our limitations and asking Allah (SWT), the Almighty and All-Knowing, for assistance.

But why does the one who made the earth and the skies and who knows all of our needs want us to ask Him? Knowing our place in the cosmos and the nature of servitude is the key to the solution. By making dua, we recognise Allah's (SWT) power and omnipotence and reclaim our position as His servants. Numerous Prophets can be found in the Quran pleading for wisdom, pardon, appreciation, and patience.

"They say, 'Our Lord! Do not let our hearts deviate after you have guided us. Grant us your mercy. You are indeed the Giver of all bounties'." (Quran 3:8)

Dua is a sign of surrender and reliance on Allah (SWT). It is a means of expressing thanks, asking for direction, and pleading with the All-Merciful for pardon, blessings, and mercy. Through dua, one can make requests for both spiritual and material needs.

Dua in times of need

When you wish to ask Allah (SWT) for daily favours or when you are in need, dua is a great way to go. But occasionally, you might have an urgent or critical need. This is where the remarkable prayer known as Salah ul Haja, or the prayer of need, enters the picture. A straightforward but effective prayer to ask the Almighty for what you desire is Salah ul Haja.

Asking for further assistance is an element of the Nawafil (supererogatory) supplication that Allah (SWT) has bestowed upon us. When you entrust your problems to Allah (SWT), you demonstrate confidence in His ability to provide for your needs.

"He who makes Wudu, and does it properly, then prays two Rakahs, Allah (SWT) will grant him whatever he may pray for, sooner or later." (Ahmad)

Method of offering Salah ul Haja

Step 1: Complete Wudu (ablution) properly.

Step 2: Pray two Rakah of Salah.

Step 3: Express gratitude to Allah (SWT) (via Dhikr, Dua, or Istighfar).

Step 4: Send blessings upon Prophet Muhammad (PBUH).

Step 5: Make the following request to Allah (SWT) sincerely:

"There is no deity but Allah, the Most Forbearing, the Ever-Generous. Glory be unto Allah, Lord of the Great Throne. Praise be to Allah, Lord of all the worlds. I ask you for those things that bring about Your mercy and Your complete forgiveness; [for] a full portion of every righteous act, and safety from every vice. Do not leave any sin of mine except that You forgive it; any anxiety except that You relieve it; nor any need of mine that pleases You except that You fulfill it, O Most Merciful of those who show mercy." (Tirmidhi)

Step 6: Tell Allah (SWT) about your requests.

You can make supplications to Allah (SWT) at any time and use the dua mentioned above to communicate your needs to Him. A sincere believer is optimistic and persistent in asking Allah (SWT) for His mercy and benefits because He loves to hear our requests and responds to them.

Harnessing the power of sincere supplications during challenging times involves turning to prayer and heartfelt invocations to seek guidance, comfort, and strength. In moments of difficulty, making sincere supplications helps individuals connect with a higher power, seeking divine intervention and solace. The act of supplication not only fosters a sense of peace and reliance on Allah (SWT) but also serves as a powerful tool for navigating through adversity, instilling hope, patience, and resilience.

Seeking solace and strength through supplications (Dua) and Quranic recitations

The Quran is the only book that can provide humans with wisdom and the means to succeed both here in this world and in the Hereafter. Dua and reciting the Quran is a direct way of communicating with Allah (SWT). As Muslims, it allows us to express our deepest fears, hopes, and desires while seeking Allah's (SWT) guidance and mercy. Let's have a look at how we can incorporate these spiritual practices into our lives:

The best source of direction from Allah (SWT) is the Quran, which provides consolation and comfort to those who are experiencing emotional pain or facing any type of hardship. It gives Muslims comfort and serenity during trying times by serving as a reminder of Allah's (SWT) kindness, compassion, and love.

The Quran instructs followers to accept the results of life's circumstances and put their faith in Allah's (SWT) plan. This trust can help people find emotional peace and let go of control over things that are out of their control, which can help reduce anxiety and concern.

The Quran further stresses how crucial it is to ask Allah (SWT) for help via prayer and supplication. It exhorts people to seek the direction, solace, and strength of Allah (SWT) during difficult times. Seeking spiritual assistance can have a significant effect.

Key Duas for Solace and Strength

It is impossible to exaggerate the significance of praying to Allah (SWT). According to the renowned Imam Ibn al-Qayyim, dua is one of the most advantageous cures.

It is the enemy of misfortune; it wards it off, heals it, keeps it from happening, and lessens or eases it when it does strike [one]. Dua is a powerful weapon for believers.

Muslims are endowed with strong and potent duas that not only alleviate stress and anxiety but also bring us closer to Allah (SWT). Incorporating these succinct yet powerful duas into your daily routine can help you remain composed and find comfort during these trying times:

Dua for Ease and Relief:

> *"O Allah, I seek refuge in You from anxiety and sorrow, weakness and laziness, miserliness and cowardice, the burden of debts, and being overpowered by men." (Sahih Bukhari)*

Dua for Patience and Perseverance:

> *"Our Lord, pour upon us patience and make our feet firm and grant us victory over the disbelieving people." (Quran 2:250)*

Dua for Strength in Hardship:

"There is no deity except You; exalted are You. Indeed, I have been of the wrongdoers." (Quran 21:87)

Dua for Relief from Anxiety

"O Allah, I ask You for beneficial knowledge, goodly provision, and acceptable deeds." (Ibn Majah)

Seeking solace and strength, we can find peace, resilience, and a deeper connection with our faith by reciting the Quran and these powerful duas.

Chapter Seven

Overcoming Adversity with Faith

Faith-Based Coping Strategies for Adversity

There are moments when our flaws and struggles become intolerable, and Allah's (SWT) tests leave us feeling hopeless and asking, "Is Allah (SWT) not listening? Why am I receiving punishment?" These are only a few of the questions that cross someone's thoughts. But the solutions we're looking for are not too far away.

Allah says in the Quran: "And your Lord says, "Call upon Me; I will respond to you." (Quran 40:60)

Our life's challenges and hardships serve as a means of putting our faith and allegiance to Allah (SWT) to the test so that we can be rewarded in this world and the next. The struggle is a normal and inevitable stage of self-improvement that all people go through as a result of a long-term process that never ends.

Our struggles do not indicate that there is a problem with us. All of these are typical stages of the process, regardless of whether we are having difficulty making ends meet, constantly fear the future, or are unsure of our identity in the world. Nothing is wrong with us.

Nothing is ever simple, never accomplished quickly, and nothing is possible without years of arduous labour. When working to build toward our dreams, we improve little by little every day and gradually move closer to our goals. Unlike running, where progress is easily measured, this improvement may not always be immediately visible or readily quantifiable.

Every difficulty we encounter is similar to a game in that we must overcome challenges to succeed. We can overcome the obstacles in our lives if we take responsibility for them.

Most people who find it difficult to overcome their obstacles believe that they are victims of their environment. Being a victim has its drawbacks: our situation has power over us, and we have no control over it. This explains why so many people experience pessimism and despair.

But Allah (SWT) wants us to connect with Him and pray. He wants us to be guided and develop our faith. He also wants us to be patient rather than argue. The bonds of our suffering suffocate us, and faith is the only way to break free. We shall, Inshallah, discover serenity as we learn to deal with and put his teachings into practice. How we handle our challenges is more of an attitude; remaining upbeat, though, is a process.

In actuality, Allah (SWT) has brought us to this point of hardship because He wants you to "change something." We are content when we are joyful. We don't alter what appears to be ideal, but when faced with a challenge, we reconsider our options and, in certain situations, are compelled to make decisions we otherwise wouldn't.

Our difficulties also highlight our strengths. We might grow from our challenges or become bitter, but as long as we seek to deepen our faith, we will emerge as better people.

As modern Muslims, we must likewise put the love of this planet at the centre of our being. We love the creation more than the creator, which leads to heartbreaks. We take for granted the gifts Allah (SWT) has bestowed upon us, including our homes, families, and friends, yet we often forget that happiness and despair are tests.

We fall so deeply in love with our possessions that we become extremely anxious every time we shatter a dish, a loved one becomes ill, we lose money, a loved one dies, or even worse, a terrible tragedy befalls us. We dread the idea of losing so much. May Allah (SWT) keep you safe!

Strengthening Iman (faith) through positive affirmations and Quranic verses

In a world full of nonstop obstacles and distractions, it is imperative that we find times of inner peace and quiet. This is where "affirmations" can work their magic to your advantage.

Positive affirmations are like seeds put in rich mental soil that can promote your spiritual development; they are not just meaningless catchphrases.

Thankfully, defining and practising positive affirmations is almost as simple as it sounds. Simply put, affirmations are statements that counteract harmful or negative beliefs. Practising them is simple: choose a phrase that reflects a positive belief and repeat it to yourself consistently.

Positive affirmations are a useful tool for self-motivation, supporting constructive life changes, and enhancing self-worth. They can help battle these often subconscious patterns of negative self-talk and replace them with more adaptable narratives if you find yourself getting caught up in them on a regular basis.

Let's take a look at some examples of positive affirmations that can help you reinforce faith:

Allah (SWT) is my Protector, and I trust in His wisdom and guidance:

> *"And whosoever puts his trust in Allah, then He will suffice him." (Quran 65:3)*

I am patient and grateful in all difficult situations:

> *"So verily, with the hardship, there is relief. Verily, with the hardship, there is relief." (Quran 94:5-6)*

I seek Allah's (SWT) forgiveness and strive to purify my heart and soul:

> *"And those who, when they commit an indecency or wrong their souls, remember Allah and ask forgiveness for their sins—and who can forgive sins except Allah?" (Quran 3:135)*

I am content with Allah's (SWT) decree, for He knows what is best for me:

> *"It may be that you dislike a thing which is good for you and that you like a thing which is bad for you. Allah knows but you do not know." (Quran 2:216)*

My faith is my strength, and I find solace in the remembrance of Allah (SWT):

> *"Verily, in the remembrance of Allah do hearts find rest." (Quran 13:28)*

I am a servant of Allah (SWT), and my purpose is to worship Him and do good deeds:

"And I did not create the jinn and mankind except to worship Me." (Quran 51:56)

Allah's (SWT) mercy and love are boundless, and I am enveloped in His care:

"My Mercy encompasses all things." (Quran 7:156)

Reciting these few affirmations regularly can help deepen your faith, enhance your spiritual resilience, and bring you closer to Allah (SWT).

Overcoming doubts and negative thoughts with Islamic teachings

As Allah (SWT) created us in such a way that it is impossible for us to remain thoughtless, we find ourselves talking to an imagined individual in our subconscious minds every single second of our lives. Our minds work like that. Our minds are among the greatest gifts that Allah (SWT) has bestowed upon us. It operates nonstop.

The best part is that it transforms into whatever we desire. Our minds can be our only allies at times. They have a tendency to mislead emotions sometimes, and even our bodies might elicit anger from them. Every emotion we experience is linked to our thoughts. Therefore, it is crucial that we comprehend our thinking.

A notion resembles a seed. We need to be mindful of whether we want a rose or a cactus growing within our heads since the more time we spend reflecting on our ideas, the larger our tree of concepts will get.

Managing our thoughts, identifying our emotions, and establishing a connection with them is essential.

Everybody has bad days. There have been times when we become mired in our thoughts and are unable to break free. We can become lost in our thoughts at times. We begin to overthink things. We begin to feel emotionally invested in hypothetical situations that never come to pass.

The majority of the suffering we experience is thought-related. Negative thoughts and self-doubt consume us. In an instant, all of the trust that has been built up over the years is gone.

Additionally, people who have known us for a while might offer their opinion, which can further impact our emotional state. However, they shouldn't have an impact on us. Because they are unaware of the years we spent fighting to get where we are, the difficulties we've encountered, and the trials that forged our patience. We will never be able to advance in life if we continue to second-guess everything we hear.

Negative thoughts can consume you constantly and never go away. You could get physical effects from them without even realising it. Knowing this will greatly assist you in taking the necessary steps to confront it and make long-term changes to your life. Below are some pointers to assist you overcome negative thinking that are based on the Quran and Sunnah and are also supported by the most recent scientific research.

- **Turn to Allah (SWT)**

When faced with negative thoughts, turning to Allah (SWT) is paramount. The Quran emphasises the power of remembrance (Dhikr) and supplication (Dua) in providing peace and solace to the heart. Through the Quran, Salah, and dua, turn to Allah (SWT). Islamic teachings demonstrate that prayer lessens anxiety and depressive symptoms.

The Prophet (PBUH) informed us that Allah (SWT) is modest and giving, and that Allah (SWT) is listening to us right now.

"He is shy that if we ask him for something that HE wouldn't give us it and He is generous because He gives us more than we ask for." (Tirmidhi)

Occasionally, the devil misleads us into believing that experiencing sadness or anxiety indicates a lack of faith or anger against us from Allah (SWT). However, this is untrue because everyone experiences sadness and anxiety as they are intuitive feelings that Allah (SWT) created in us.

Therefore, it is important to realise that we are resilient and that Allah (SWT) empowers us to conquer any obstacles in our path. We frequently underestimate our own strength and resilience, but Allah (SWT) is aware of that.

Thus, ask Allah (SWT) with confidence that He is listening to you and will answer. Make a dua. Spend some time meditating and reciting the Quran. The Quran is a heart healer, according to Allah (SWT), who also describes it as a healing. Even just one verse should be read from the Quran every day.

The Sunnah also encourages believers to seek refuge in Allah (SWT) during times of distress.

The Prophet Muhammad (PBUH) often made supplications like, "O Allah, I seek refuge in You from anxiety and grief, weakness and laziness, miserliness and cowardice, the burden of debts, and from being overpowered by men." (Sahih Bukhari)

- **Think positively**

Focus on the positive, and you will find that it will grow and thrive. We are all extremely fortunate, but the Shaytan (devil) speaks softly and manipulates us to focus only on the negative aspects of our existence and ignore all the positive aspects. Thus, focus on the positive and genuinely seek it out. Consider your blessings and express your gratitude for them.

> *The Prophet (PBUH) said: "No fatigue, nor disease, nor sorrow, nor sadness, nor hurt, nor distress befalls a Muslim, even it were a prick he receives from a thorn, but Allah expiates some of his sins for that." (Sahih Bukhari)*

When you're going through a difficult period, and you can't think of anything positive in your life, remember that your sins are being forgiven! And keep in mind what Allah (SWT) declares:

> *"If you are grateful, I will give you more." (Quran 14:7)*

- **Employ affirmations**

It is a truth that everything we say and do on a daily basis gets ingrained in our subconscious. Even under challenging circumstances, we can change the course of events by speaking positively to ourselves. Therefore, we must develop the habit of feeding our minds with positive energy by employing affirmations. It will eventually seep into our subconscious and we'll begin to believe it.

Remember that the sun rises every day, regardless of how dark the night is. As challenging as it may be, we must endure with patience and gratitude. Unfathomable rewards will follow these difficult times, making the struggle worthwhile.

- **Put your hope and trust In Allah (SWT)**

Have faith in Allah (SWT). Have faith that things will turn around. And sincerely hope that everything you do will bring you Baraka from Allah (SWT). Give Him abundant thanks. Whatever you ask of him, by His mercy, He will give it to you.

- **Don't strive for excellence**

Everything in this world strives to become steadier; it is a fact. Everyone strives for greater excellence. However, there are moments when our quest for perfection causes us to think negatively. The definition of perfection includes having the ideal voice, accent, body type, appearance, and attire, among other things.

Just as we have no influence over the colour of our eyes or the form of our faces, we also have to acknowledge that some things are beyond our control. Thus, it is a waste of time and energy to think negatively and attempt to influence external factors.

Discover the hidden skills and vibrant gifts Allah (SWT) has bestowed upon you, and express your gratitude. Defy all that negativity and surround yourself with the world's most exquisite hues.

Follow your interests and maintain an optimistic outlook at all times. The most crucial thing to remember is to complete everything in your own unique manner.

Since everyone is unique, at the end of the day, it's important to learn how to control your thoughts, comprehend who you are, and create a mindful connection with Allah (SWT).

By integrating spiritual practices into your daily life, you can strengthen your relationship with Allah (SWT). This, in turn, can help overcome negative thinking and foster a more positive outlook on life.

Transforming Challenges into Opportunities for Growth

With all of His wisdom, Allah (SWT) has created a world full of difficulties and hardships. He has assured us that no one will ever find perfection in this world, called Dunya.

Adversity is a necessary aspect of life for everyone, regardless of age, money, health, or morality. Remember that hardships are universal, and Islam teaches us how to meet them head-on with faith, resiliency, and resolve.

You'll be better off seeing obstacles as chances for personal development because they are an unavoidable aspect of life. In the face of unforeseen challenges, you always have an option. When faced with challenges, you have two options: either turn away from the situation or use it as motivation to reach your goals.

These are the times when the old certainties end, and the seeds of growth are planted. Let's explore how you might use the unforeseen obstacles you face as building blocks to become a stronger, more competent version of yourself.

When we look closely at our own lives, we may see the many difficulties we encounter. There is no distinction made by these trials between virtue, money, or health. They cover a broad spectrum of situations, such as dealing with challenging coworkers, supervisors, or family members, as well as losing one's job or having financial difficulties. Deeply personal struggles could include an unfulfilled love, an unworkable financial load, an unsuccessful marriage, or social tensions with in-laws and other family members.

As Muslims, we must understand that Allah (SWT) is constantly aware of our situation. We should never question Allah's (SWT) presence or concern for us, as He perceives and comprehends everything that happens to us.

To highlight this point, the Prophet Muhammad (PBUH) once likened Allah's (SWT) benevolence to a mother's affection for her child. Like a mother would never cast her kid into the flames, so too does Allah (SWT) show more mercy and concern for His creation than any human could ever know.

The Prophet Muhammad (PBUH) said, "Allah is more merciful to His slaves than a mother is to her child." (Sahih Bukhari)

According to the Islamic perspective, every difficulty, test, or hardship a believer faces is an opportunity to draw closer to Allah (SWT), strengthen one's faith, and develop a resilient character. Let's examine it in detail!

Embracing hardship as a catalyst for personal and spiritual development

When you recognise the value of personal development, you'll come to realise that it's essential to turn fresh obstacles into chances for betterment.

It's about realising that every obstacle you encounter presents a chance for personal development, learning, and goal achievement—becoming a better version of yourself.

When you welcome change in your personal life, you provide yourself access to fresh viewpoints, experiences, and abilities that will enable you to face challenges head-on and triumph over them with fortitude and assurance.

A lifetime of self-improvement and self-discovery can increase prosperity, pleasure, and fulfilment.

When faced with obstacles, it is vital to have unwavering confidence in Allah (SWT). We must never give up on His mercy and wisdom, no matter how big or how bad the issue is. We should remember the accounts of the Prophets who never lost faith in Allah's (SWT) kindness when faced with adversity.

Problems should not be seen as insurmountable barriers but as chances for personal growth. Allah (SWT) warns us that until we change, He will not alter our circumstances. As a result, every obstacle allows us to think, grow, and change as people.

It is not in the good times that we truly measure our worth as people; rather, it is in the way we respond to hardship and difficulties. Life's challenges are not to break us but to strengthen us.

Even when faced with obstacles that appear insurmountable, we should constantly be guided by our faith and optimistic outlooks.

It's critical to resist allowing issues to control our feelings and thoughts when they arise. Instead of letting obstacles lead us, we ought to be directed by our goals, ambitions, and unshakeable faith in Allah (SWT). Issues are there to be solved, not to dominate our lives. Ignoring issues won't make them disappear; we must face and address them.

Challenges inevitably arise in life and impact each of us as individuals and as a community. As Muslims, we must face these difficulties with resolute faith, fortitude, and the conviction that Allah's (SWT) will is always motivated by His wisdom and mercy.

Issues should spur us on to become better versions of ourselves rather than lead us. Recall that ease follows every hardship, and we can conquer obstacles by placing our trust in Allah (SWT).

Embracing challenges through faith-based perspectives

This perspective involves recognising that challenges are an inherent part of the human experience and serve a higher purpose. Here are some key insights from a faith-based viewpoint:

- **Finding personal development and adaptability in the face of misery**

Despite being unwanted and frequently painful, adversity has a transforming force that makes our inner strength and perseverance truly apparent. When we take on obstacles head-on while maintaining our faith, we find hidden reserves of strength that could have lain dormant otherwise.

Every challenge turns into a chance to develop self and character. We learn to rely on Allah (SWT) via the furnace of hardship, receiving strength from His unfailing love and grace.

We emerge from the crucible of hardship more robust more resilient, and reshaped through tenacity and unflinching faith.

- **Having faith in Allah's (SWT) sovereignty**

Relying on Allah's (SWT) sovereignty is a significant act of giving up control over our own goals, plans, and aspirations in favour of the Creator's superior knowledge and heavenly design.

It's an admission that His design is far greater than what we can comprehend as humans.

We realise that His flawless plan is not limited by time or situation when we give up control and put all our faith in Him. By doing this, we find comfort in the knowledge that He has a reason for our suffering and that, despite everything, He is at work in the background, transforming us into expressions of His grace and love.

- **Discovering unwavering hope in Allah's (SWT) promises**

The promises of Allah (SWT) provide us with a steadfast anchor of hope amidst the ups and downs of life. In the depths of darkness, his promises of unending love, steadfast protection, and plentiful provision shine brightly. Every promise He makes gives us the fortitude and self-assurance to tackle hardship head-on. We take comfort in knowing He is loyal, even in the face of seemingly hopeless situations, since we have grounded our hope in His unwavering character and irrefutable promises. Our hope turns into a solid rock we can stand on in the face of the raging storms surrounding us.

- **Taking solace in Allah's (SWT) presence**

It brings comfort to know that Allah (SWT) is always there to assist, guide, and console us during life's turbulent storms when the waters seem destined to swallow us whole. By praying, meditating, and reflecting to locate His consoling presence, we might find strength in the deepest depths of despair.

He envelops us in His tender embrace as we give Him access to our hearts, filling us with a calm beyond our comprehension. We find refuge in the depths of His presence, knowing that we are never alone and that the minute elements of our lives are being carefully arranged for our ultimate benefit by His divine providence.

When we trust in Allah's (SWT) divine plan, it allows us to face life's challenges with grace, resiliency, and steadfast confidence. It makes it possible for us to see obstacles as transforming chances for development and learning. We can fulfill our mission and be strengthened by His unwavering love when we link our hearts with His.

We accomplish this by following His unbounded wisdom. We walk hand in hand with our Creator through the valleys and the peaks of life, finding strength in His purpose and promises. We set out on a path of empowerment, travelling in strength, fulfilment, and purpose when we embrace His perfect design.

Chapter Eight

Maintaining Emotional Wellness

Understanding Emotional Resilience in Islam

At some point in our lives, we may experience emotional crises that are difficult to handle. These crises can stem from different causes, and often lead to behavioural, emotional, physical, and mental discomfort. The capacity to overcome suffering, adjust to change, and preserve mental health in the face of adversity is known as resilience. For many Muslims, perseverance and mental health are greatly aided by their religion.

The Quran and Sunnah offer a wealth of wisdom that can help us get through these difficult times by offering support, stability, resources, and help. Muslims are encouraged by the Quran to develop strong resilience that perseveres through hardships.

"Indeed, those who have said, 'Our Lord is Allah' and then remained steadfast—the angels will descend upon them, [saying], 'Do not fear and do not grieve but receive good tidings of Paradise, which you were promised.'"
(Quran 41:30)

This reassures Muslims that fear and grief, which are negative emotions, do not solve problems and should not stand in the way of progress. The instruction provided by the Quran teaches Muslims to always be strong, to meet life's obstacles head-on, and to do so without complaining or growing weary. As the Quran envisions, a community capable of facing life's challenges with courage and dignity is fostered by this moderation and balance.

Islam provides a comprehensive framework for dealing with emotional challenges. The teachings of Islam emphasise patience, gratitude, and trust in Allah's (SWT) wisdom. These spiritual practices help individuals manage stress and maintain emotional balance. Understanding emotional resilience in Islam is important, so let's examine how it can be achieved.

Managing emotions (Ahwal) with mindfulness and self-awareness

Ahwal (emotional states) involves recognising and comprehending the nature of emotional and psychological conditions that Muslims experience. One way of doing this is through mindfulness. Mindfulness is the state or quality of being conscious or aware of something; more precisely, it is a mental state attained as a therapeutic technique by focusing on the present moment while quietly recognising and embracing one's feelings, ideas and bodily sensations.

Islam emphasises mindfulness as a core component of the religion. Muslims are urged to practice mindfulness in all facets of their lives, such as everyday activities, relationships, and prayers. Believers should try to be conscious of Allah's (SWT) presence at all times, as the Quran teaches that He is ever-present and aware.

Mindfulness can reduce stress and bad emotions and foster well-being. As mindfulness is ingrained in Islam, it is incorporated into daily rituals like Dhikr and prayer. By engaging in mindfulness practices,

Muslims can enhance their mental and physical well-being and develop a stronger sense of connectedness to Allah (SWT).

In Islamic tradition, mindfulness is associated with the virtue of Muraqabah, a word whose basic meaning is "to watch, observe, regard attentively." When Muslims are in a condition of Muraqabah, they are constantly aware that Allah (SWT) is cognizant of them both inside and externally.

It is a full and vigilant state of self-awareness in one's body, intellect, and heart relationship with Allah (SWT). The foundation of Muraqabah is the understanding that Allah (SWT) is constantly keeping an eye on us. As a result, we learn to pay more attention to and care for our own deeds, thoughts, feelings, and interior states of being.

Remembering Allah (SWT) is one way that Islamic activities use mindfulness. In addition to helping believers concentrate their thoughts on Allah and His teachings, this practice calms the body and mind.

Islam also emphasises awareness through the idea of Tawakkul, or having faith in Allah (SWT). It entails accepting that Allah (SWT) is our ultimate source of guidance and control and trusting in His plan for our life. Muslims who practice this can relax and stop worrying about the future, allowing them to concentrate on the here and now.

The acquisition of Muraqabah for one's Lord—who is so glorious and exalted that it is as though one is seeing Him—produces the means leading to stillness (Al-Sakinah), which leads to contentment in this life, in addition to the reward of eternal Paradise in the Hereafter.

To truly grasp the essence and importance of mindfulness in Islam, it is crucial to understand its key elements:

Tadabbur is the practice of reflecting deeply and pursuing wisdom through knowledge. The first element of Tadabbur entails learning something in order to comprehend the reality and applying that understanding to your daily life. It emphasises discerning between useful and irrelevant information. Tadabbur is the philosophy of letting go of the irrelevant details and concentrating on what is significant, accurate, and pertinent.

> *"Do they not reflect upon the Word (the Quran), or has anything come to them that did not come to their forefathers?" (Quran 23:68)*

Tafakkur involves thinking critically about what is currently known and grasping it from several angles. You can better grasp what you've learned for lifetime learning by reflecting on it. Self-reflection exercises such as meditation help you eliminate negative thoughts from your mind.

> *The Prophet Muhammad (PBUH) said, "The one who shows you your faults is your friend. The one who pays you lip service and pretends to be your friend is your enemy." (Sahih Bukhari)*

Tasabbur means endurance. After gaining knowledge, it is essential to cultivate gratitude for what you have and to remain patient and consistent in your efforts. It inspires you to do more good while bringing inner calm and fulfillment. The belief that everything occurs for a purpose and is a gift from God sustains patience. Given that people are unaware of concealed plans, it is best to exercise patience in the face of hardship and express gratitude for what we have.

> *The Messenger of Allah (PBUH) said, "How wonderful is the case of a believer. There is good for him in everything, and this applies only to a believer. If prosperity comes to him, he thanks Allah, and that is good for him.*

If adversity befalls him, he endures it patiently, and that is also good for him." (Sahih Muslim)

Tazkiyah is an Arabic term meaning purification. It alludes to the purification of the heart in this context. Refusing to allow your five senses to poison your heart is the greatest method to adhere to this crucial mindfulness tenet.

It is vital to pay attention to the five senses because they have an impact on the spiritual heart. Let nothing except happiness, calmness, and tranquillity enter your thoughts and heart. Give up on any other ideas that are upsetting your inner peace.

Regular fasting, expressing thanks, abstaining from hurting people verbally or physically, and making wise financial and time decisions are some ways to achieve this. These pursuits keep your heart pure and only result in serenity for both you and others.

"Has the time not come for those who have believed that their hearts should become humble at the remembrance of Allah and what has come down of the truth, and that they not be like those who were given the Scripture before, and a long period passed over them, so their hearts hardened? And many of them are defiantly disobedient." (Quran 57:16)

Tashirukkur, which means thankfulness, is the fifth element. Look around you, and you will discover a plethora of things for which you should be grateful. You have many resources and relationships in addition to everyday needs that help you with your daily tasks. Being humble is maintained by regularly expressing gratitude for the blessings in your life. It helps you to value your life and keeps you from feeling proud of yourself.

"And if you should count the favours of Allah (SWT), you could not enumerate them. Indeed, Allah is Forgiving and Merciful." (Quran 16:18)

Taqwa: The final element is a result of the previous five elements. It alludes to piety and divinity that support you in all circumstances. Taqwa can be attained by abiding by Islamic teachings, practising good deeds, and refraining from evil.

The Prophet Muhammad (PBUH) said, "Fear Allah (SWT) wherever you are. Follow up a bad deed with a good deed to erase it, and engage others with beautiful character."(Sahih Bukhari)

However, there are many advantages to being conscious of our feelings. When we know our emotions, we can successfully synchronise our intentions and actions. We have more control and influence over our behaviours as we know what we are going through and what our intentions are. We feel more in control of our lives and are less prone to be perplexed by our actions.

Being self-aware leads to confidence, and having confidence in oneself entails understanding the positive traits Allah (SWT) has bestowed upon you and making the necessary efforts to achieve your goals. If you abuse it, you will deny yourself the gifts that Allah (SWT) has bestowed upon you and become full of conceit.

Comprehending the significance of self-awareness in Islam is crucial for an individual's spiritual development and relationship with Allah (SWT). Being self-aware in Islam entails more than simply admitting one's mistakes; it also entails attentive presence and in-depth reflection.

You can develop a deeper understanding of your thoughts, feelings, and behaviours by practising self-awareness. Through introspection, you can grow personally and spiritually by identifying areas for growth.

To maintain emotion well-being as a Muslim, we must learn to control our emotions. This includes learning how to deal with rage and how to deal with calmness. Delving into Islamic teachings and providing mental health and well-being education help us better comprehend and regulate our emotions. Anger, in particular, has a powerful influence on mental health and well-being, especially in the Muslim community.

The Hadith and Quran place a strong emphasis on the need to control one's anger, highlighting the virtues of self-control, patience, and forgiveness. These lessons serve as beacons of light, providing a clear road map for navigating the complexity of rage and how it affects mental health. By incorporating these lessons into daily life, Muslims can become more resilient, which in turn promotes inner serenity and robust mental health and well-being.

Coping Strategies for Stress and Anxiety

Everyone experiences stress and anxiety from time to time. Anxiety can take on diverse forms and affect individuals to differing degrees, but one thing is certain: even when anxiety seems uncontrollable, there are strategies to deal with it. Of course, as Muslims, we must turn to Islamic teachings for support if anxiety is interfering with our daily lives and preventing us from being productive. Let's have a look at these effective strategies!

Implementing relaxation techniques (Tafakkur) and spiritual breathing exercises

Implementing relaxation techniques, particularly Tafakkur (deep contemplation), can effectively address stress and anxiety. Tafakkur involves reflective thinking, allowing individuals to deeply explore their thoughts and feelings. By setting aside quiet time for this practice, one can gain perspective, reduce mental clutter, and cultivate inner peace.

This technique encourages mindfulness and self-awareness, helping to identify stressors and evaluate their impact calmly. Regular Tafakkur can shift focus from overwhelming worries to a balanced, grounded state of mind. It also fosters a deeper connection with oneself and one's surroundings, promoting emotional resilience.

Integrating Tafakkur into daily routines, along with other relaxation techniques such as deep breathing or meditation, can enhance overall well-being and alleviate symptoms of anxiety, leading to a more harmonious and tranquil life.

Similarly, spiritual breathing is another effective coping technique. In this practice, we "exhale" by admitting our guilt, acknowledging our sins, and expressing gratitude to Allah (SWT) for His forgiveness – this is the act of confession. Afterwards, we "inhale" by surrendering ourselves over to Allah (SWT) once more. Giving up control of our life to Allah (SWT) and putting our faith in the Holy Spirit to guide and enable us is known as surrender.

Seeking refuge in Allah (Istihadha) from overwhelming emotions

In Islam, Istihadha (flowing blood) is understood as a disruption in a woman's menstrual cycle, preventing her from performing certain religious acts of worship (Ibadah). Istihadha is not the same as Hayz (menstruation); it is considered a form of Najasat (impurity). A woman experiencing Istihadha is still required to pray, but for her prayers to be heard, she must perform the necessary deeds.

Let's look at the guidelines she must follow to perform her Salah correctly.

Qalilah (Light): Every time she prays, a woman with Istihadha Qalilah must perform Wudu (ablution) and change her sanitary towel. If the sanitary towel has not become Najis (impure), it does not need to be replaced.

Mutawassitah (Moderate): In addition to changing her sanitary towel and performing Wudu during each Salah, a woman with Istihadha Mutawassitah must also conduct a Ghusl (shower) before the Fajr (dawn) prayer.

Kathirah (Heavy): A woman with Istihadha Kathirah is required to conduct three Ghusls (the first before dawn prayer, the second before noon plus afternoon prayers and the third before evening as well as night prayers). She must also replace her sanitary towels before every Salah. A woman who has Istihadha Kathirah is not required to perform Wudu for every Salah; the Ghusl is adequate in this regard.

To express seeking refuge in Allah (SWT) from overwhelming emotions, Muslim women can use the following supplications:

General Istiadhah: *"I seek refuge in Allah (SWT) from the accursed devil."*

Specific for Anxiety and Overwhelming Emotions: *"O Allah (SWT), I seek refuge in You from anxiety and sorrow, weakness and laziness, miserliness and cowardice, the burden of debts, and the overpowering of men."*

This supplication asks for protection from various forms of emotional distress and difficulties, seeking solace in Allah (SWT).

By cultivating patience, gratitude, and self-awareness, Muslims can manage stress, anxiety, and emotional crises effectively. These practices help maintain mental well-being, deepen their connection with Allah (SWT), and foster inner peace and resilience.

Chapter Nine

Seeking Knowledge and Wisdom

Importance of Seeking Knowledge in Islam

As it is said that "power comes from knowledge" since Allah's (SWT) initial revelation to our beloved Holy Prophet (PBUH), the Quran has stressed the significance of acquiring knowledge in Islam. Regardless of their gender, age, nationality, social class, or anything else, all Muslims have a duty to pursue knowledge.

As liberating Muslims, we all have an equal right to education and the pursuit of knowledge for our own advancement and empowerment.

Islam values knowledge acquisition as a virtue. Numerous passages in the Quran exhort us to use our minds and reflect on things. The following verse is one example:

"And He has subjected to you whatever is in the heavens and whatever is on the earth - all from Him. Indeed in that are signs for people who give thought." (Quran 45:13)

One unique quality that sets humanity apart from many other creations is our capacity to think critically, reflect, and learn beyond our innate inclinations. Through knowledge, we transcend our baser selves to that which is flawless and dignified through knowledge.

What is knowledge in Islam?

Islamic teachings place a high importance on knowledge, which includes comprehension of the Quran and Hadith, as well as insights gained via study, experience, observation, or divine revelation. In other words, knowledge in Islam includes everything that can be understood about any given topic.

The Prophet Muhammad (PBUH) presented himself as a lifelong student and educator who would always stress the importance of getting an education that would help not just his own family but also the families of his companions and the Muslim community as a whole.

> *One well-known hadith that Abu Hurairah recounts describes how the Prophet Muhammad (PBUH) inspired those around him; "Whoever takes a path upon which to obtain knowledge, Allah makes the path to Paradise easy for him." (Tirmidhi)*

Knowledge acquisition has always been regarded as a necessary component of human existence, and Muslims view the pursuit of knowledge as a basic duty. Let's examine!

Embracing lifelong learning and personal development

Islam emphasises the value of knowledge acquisition as a way to deepen one's religion, accelerate personal development, and make a constructive contribution to society. For all Muslims, acquiring knowledge is a lifetime endeavour that is vital because education enables them to comprehend their faith, themselves, and the world more fully. Islamic beliefs are strongly ingrained in the idea of lifelong learning since Muslims are obligated by their faith to pursue knowledge throughout their lives.

The significance of knowledge is emphasised in multiple passages of the Quran, including "And say: 'My Lord, increase me in knowledge.'" (Quran 20:114)

Islam encourages us to pursue knowledge throughout our entire life and be lifelong learners. Not only is acquiring knowledge a moral and religious duty, but it is also an ongoing one.

The light of religion ignites an insatiable thirst for study and comprehension of both the secrets of nature and divine revelation. While spiritual knowledge, especially what is necessary for Muslims to follow correctly, is of great importance, we must also seek scientific understanding that can advance humanity as a whole and uplift our society. In contrast, the darkness of unbelief, on the other hand, causes an endless thirst for material possessions, money, and fleeting pleasures at the price of the soul itself.

No matter how much knowledge a person possesses, they are ignorant if they believe they don't need to acquire more. Acknowledging our perpetual thirst for knowledge is a humble gesture. In actuality, there is a clear correlation between a person's humility and wisdom ratio.

Every Muslim should approach life with the mindset that even as teachers, we are all lifelong learners and we should be humble enough to pick up knowledge from everyone, no matter their position in society. Learning is a talent, but the willingness to learn is a conscious decision. Islam encourages this decision in each and every one of us, urging us to become lifelong learners. Developing a habit requires us to go deeper and learn more about not only the world but also ourselves. It aids in our comprehension of what is actually happening and gives us the ability to recognise deceit and deception and see the world through realistic windows.

It makes it easier for us to put our truer desires into words, meaningfully satisfying our unique contributions. All of this is possible because Allah (SWT) gave each and every one of us a brain capable of infinite learning. This is what makes all people capable of being geniuses. Whether we choose to make use of it or ignore it out of ignorance is entirely up to us.

In addition, personal development is an ongoing process that calls for constant learning, progress, and self-improvement. To fulfil our potential and succeed in all facets of life, we must broaden our knowledge, abilities, and viewpoints. The essential idea of welcoming growth is at the core of personal development.

Self-improvement and personal development are essential to living a fulfilling life. It's a path of self-exploration, never-ending education, and accepting fresh viewpoints. By taking an active role in our own personal development, we can realise our full potential and design a meaningful existence.

The Quran highlights the importance of taking active steps in personal development and self-improvement to bring about positive change. In the Quran, Allah (SWT) says:

> *"Indeed, Allah (SWT) will not change the condition of a people until they change what is in themselves." (Quran 13:11)*

It is our duty as Muslims to constantly work toward bettering ourselves in both our spiritual and material lives. While our beloved Prophet (PBUH) counselled us to be the greatest versions of ourselves, Allah (SWT) urges us to grow and develop. It is even more important for us to take charge of our personal development in a world full of obstacles and a pressing demand for change.

We must better ourselves in many ways, such as embracing more Islamic practices or elevating secular facets of our lives, to assist us in navigating the difficulties of this life and carrying out our Islamic duties. This is due to the fact that accepting personal transformation not only helps ourselves but also the environment in which we live.

Let's examine some essential ideas and methods that will enable you to set out on your own life-changing path.

Lifelong Learning: Adopt a growth mentality and make learning a lifelong commitment. To broaden your horizons and acquire fresh insights, indulge in reading books, tuning into podcasts, and participating in webinars or workshops. Look for mentors or role models who can help you along the way and motivate you. Ask inquiries, remain curious, and be willing to learn new things. Accepting lifelong learning promotes personal development and keeps you flexible in a changing world.

Building Self-Awareness: Personal development is based on self-awareness. It entails gaining a profound comprehension of our feelings, ideas, virtues, and shortcomings. Give yourself some time to think and contemplate. You can discover important insights by exploring your inner landscape through meditation or mindfulness exercises. Gaining self-awareness will enable you to make decisions that align with who you are.

Establishing Insightful Objectives: Establish measurable objectives consistent with your values sand areas of passion. Divide them into more manageable, smaller steps. Make a vision board or write reminders to help you stay focused on your objectives. As you advance, revisit and modify your goals frequently, acknowledging your accomplishments along the way. Recall that the journey is just as significant as the destination.

Accepting Difficulties and Being Resilient: On the road to personal growth, obstacles and failures are unavoidable. Accept them as chances for personal development rather than running away from them. Take calculated chances, push yourself beyond your comfort zone, and learn from your mistakes.

Reframe failures as opportunities for learning to strengthen your resilience. Create coping mechanisms by taking care of yourself, keeping up a support system, and adopting an optimistic outlook. Recall that it is by overcoming obstacles that we find our own strength.

So, recall that self-improvement is an ongoing process that calls for commitment, endurance, and introspection. You'll uncover new aspects of yourself and realise your full potential with every step you take forward. Accept the journey and allow your personal growth to serve as the impetus for a fulfilling existence.

The Benefits of Seeking True Knowledge

Prophet Muhammad (PBUH) said: "One who proceeds on a path in the pursuit of knowledge, God makes him proceed therewith on a path to the Garden (Paradise). And, verily, the angels spread their wings for the seekers of knowledge out of delight. Verily, every creature of the heaven and the earth asks forgiveness for the seeker of knowledge, even the fish in the sea. The merit of the 'alim (the learned) over the 'abid (the devout) is like the merit of the moon over the stars on a full moon night. The learned are the heirs of the prophets, for the prophets did not leave behind a legacy of wealth but that of knowledge. So whoever partakes of it derives copious benefit." (Sunah Abu Dawood)

Knowledge is obtained with pure, altruistic, and divine intent; it changes a person's personality and makes them celestial. A person with such understanding becomes the personification of qualities inspired by Allah (SWT), and his behaviour, words, and character make these qualities evident.

It is a virtue to seek knowledge through the appropriate channels. It offers the seeker a lot of benefits. Put another way, learning can be attained sincerely rather than requiring one to be a highly competent scholar.

Allah (SWT) not only rewards the good deed of pursuing knowledge but also honours those who possess it. In the Quran, Allah (SWT) praises those who have attained it and raises their status. It is crucial to remember that Allah (SWT) is the one who elevates and debases individuals.

Simply because we are on the path of learning does not give us the right to think that we are better than others or to treat them with contempt. We appreciate Allah's (SWT) favours bestowed upon us. Allah (SWT) is indeed all-knowing.

One benefit of knowledge is that it can inspire other virtues, such as genuine fear and reverence for Allah (SWT). The more knowledge we acquire, the more moral and modest we should all be. These are a few benefits that have resulted from pursuing knowledge.

> *"It is those of His servants who have knowledge who stand in true awe of Allah (SWT). Indeed Allah (SWT) is almighty, most forgiving." (Quran 35:28)*

Acquiring knowledge and learning new things are necessary, but they shouldn't be done all at once. Throughout the process, one should be patient and have a strong intention. Achieving certain things could be easier than others. Remember that if someone attempts to study, even if it is difficult for them, Allah (SWT) will reward them double for their efforts because of their diligence in pursuing knowledge. Allah's (SWT) wealth is truly boundless.

Thus, seeking true knowledge in Islam is a noble pursuit that brings numerous benefits. It draws a person closer to Allah (SWT), as knowledge is valued highly in the Quran and Sunnah. It guides one to practice their faith correctly and make informed decisions. Moreover, the pursuit of knowledge is an act of worship, promising eternal rewards in the Hereafter.

The Essence of Wisdom: Understanding and Application in Life

All men desire to carry out their duties with discernment and understanding. Of course, what wisdom actually means is a perplexing question. Nearly everyone has a different definition of wisdom and a desire to acquire it via a lengthy and difficult journey.

The general definition of wisdom is having a deep understanding of others, events, or circumstances, which leads to the capacity to make decisions or take actions that consistently yield desired outcomes. Terms like sagacity, discernment, or insights are frequently used interchangeably with the word wisdom.

Wisdom is a hidden capacity for logic and thinking (Aql in Arabic). Through the known realities, it uncovers unknown ones. Wisdom uses reasonable induction and deduction reasoning to establish logical norms. Based on these logical principles, wisdom then draws conclusions and outcomes that are beneficial.

The Quran places a strong emphasis on using wisdom in all areas, such as learning about Allah (SWT), life after death, historical interpretation, relationships between different religions, good and evil knowledge, justice and injustice, autonomy and oppression, the nature of this world, morality and immorality, and the meaning of this life.

The Prophet Muhammad (PBUH) said, "Actions are but by intentions" (Sahih Bukhari)

These teachings stress the significance of intention and knowledge in personal growth and ethical living.

Applying Islamic Principles to Decision-Making

Every person must regularly make decisions for both their professional and personal demands. Making decisions is one of the crucial but labour-intensive processes. It is a fundamental aspect of life on Earth. It is the responsibility of every Muslim to consider Islamic teachings when making decisions that will not negatively impact humanity or society at large.

People frequently make snap decisions which they later regret. Making decisions without consulting others or using reasoned judgment frequently has a detrimental effect on one's life. Others in the neighbourhood where people reside are also impacted. A poor judgment, or a decision based on faulty reasoning, can have dire repercussions. Islam also advises using reason and critical thinking while making decisions.

But since there are a lot of variables involved in each decision, it also makes sense to deliberate before making one. Hence, before making a decision, every Muslim should use caution and diligence.

Islam, as a holistic lifestyle, provides insightful advice on how to approach making decisions and emphasises the value of commitment after a decision is made. A productive Muslim is one who is decisive, as progress in life can only be achieved by well-considered decision-making.

"Whoever seeks a decision through my tradition (Sunnah) and does not find it, let him act according to what is in the Quran." (Sahih Muslim)

Step-by-step process for arriving at wise decisions

Consider: You'd be shocked at how many individuals make decisions without giving them much thought! Furthermore, thinking does not imply looking at the ceiling for a few minutes in hopes of having an epiphany! Thinking is coming up with ideas, analysing them, applying your experience to determine the best course of action, and carefully considering the effects of your choice.

Investigate/Consult: Take a look around, inquire, consult others, get feedback from family and friends, and truly use every resource at your disposal to fully grasp the ramifications of your choice.

Perform Istikhara: Allah (SWT) is incredibly gracious to us; seeing that it would be difficult for us to make decisions, He made unique channels of communication available for us to use while making judgments. We have already covered the Istikhara prayer in a previous section of this book.

Choose/Action: After giving it some thought, consulting with others, and—above all—pleading with Allah (SWT) for direction through an Istikhara prayer, what should you do next? Make a choice! Act now! And act decisively, making every initial move you can think of to ensure that you are unable to change your mind!

Dua or Tawakkul: Even after you've decided and taken some action, the process isn't finished. Offer prayers and put your faith in Allah (SWT). Even if you may have made the right choice, remember that making the right decisions requires a lot of dua and faith in Allah (SWT) therefore keep going!

"And when you have decided, then rely upon Allah. Indeed, Allah loves those who rely (upon Him)." (Quran 42:38)

"And whoever submits his face (himself) to Allah (SWT) while he is a believer, he has grasped the most trustworthy handhold. And to Allah (SWT) return all matters for decision." (Quran 3:159)

Making decisions is difficult, but rather than avoiding them and paying the price in this life and the next, strengthen your ability to make decisions by using the following techniques to make decisions on a daily basis. No matter how big or small the decision, simply take action!

From an Islamic perspective, the decision-making process can greatly advance one's career and personal development. Through the adoption of these tenets, individuals can develop a mentality that fosters analytical reasoning, deliberate decision-making, and the capacity to navigate the outcomes of their decisions. Muslims who adopt this idea will be able to strengthen their resilience, have more faith in Allah's (SWT) plan, and comprehend the rationale for their choices on a deeper level.

Allah (SWT) ordered the Prophet (PBUH) to employ the quality of Hikma to convey assurance during life's uncertainties, lead the lost, and resurrect dead hearts. In addition to requiring a great degree of knowledge when striving to resurrect barren souls, the Holy Prophet Muhammad (PBUH) was also the epitome of wisdom in his life, handling all the difficulties and doubts he encountered when he began calling people to Allah's (SWT) path.

Through the Divine revelations to His chosen messengers, whom He commanded to impart and reflect His wisdom (Hikmah) to people, Allah (SWT) revealed the ultimate wisdom or intellect.

Allah (SWT) instructed Prophet Muhammad (PBUH): "Invite to the way of your Lord with Hikma and kind teaching." (Quran 16:125)

Chapter Ten

Strengthening Relationships & Community Support

Role of Social Support in Building Resilience

It's a given that we'll encounter obstacles and disappointments along the way. We come to fully appreciate the importance of social support considering that it can significantly impact our wellbeing during these times. People gain from social support in many ways, since it acts as a safety net to assist them deal with life's challenges.

Our lives are significantly impacted by our social relationships. These relationships may be with friends, relatives, coworkers, or even strangers. Their strength lies at the core of our social network. The quality and quantity of these relationships can have a significant impact on our ability to bounce back from setbacks and maintain overall mental health.

Good social ties are positively correlated with both psychological and physical well-being, making them an obvious winning strategy in life. It follows that social connections are important for resilience and that this is partly because they reduce stress during difficult times.

Fostering strong relationships

In Islam, forming wholesome relationships is very important. For the purpose of Allah (SWT), we are commanded by our faith to cultivate solid and wholesome relationships based on love, respect, and compassion for others.

Our lives are significantly impacted by the intimate interactions we have with our loved ones. These relationships give us emotional support, company, and a feeling of belonging. They support, uplift, and inspire us as we face life's obstacles.

In Islam, familial ties hold great importance. For the sake of Allah (SWT), we are urged to establish relationships grounded in love, respect, and compassion. These connections, guided by our faith, support our own development and growth while fostering harmony and togetherness within our community.

Developing good relationships takes patience, persistence, and commitment over the course of a lifetime. But we may create deep bonds that strengthen our community and bring us closer to Allah (SWT) by using good communication, kindness, understanding, and compassion.

Providing mutual support and encouragement during difficult times

Mutual support involves offering help and encouragement in both small and significant ways. This can range from simply listening to actively participating in each other's lives and offering practical assistance. Encouragement during difficult times helps individuals feel understood and valued, reinforcing their resilience.

Being available for others, whether through a listening ear, a helping hand, or emotional support, creates a reciprocal relationship where both parties benefit from the interaction. This reciprocal support system not only aids in overcoming immediate challenges but also fosters long-term resilience and well-being.

Effective ways to build strong relationships

Therefore, maintaining good connections can positively impact not only ourselves but also the people around us and profoundly affect numerous facets of our lives. So, how can one establish these kinds of relationships?

At the core of every healthy relationship lies love and kindness. Islam emphasises the significance of fostering these qualities in all relationships, including family, marriage, friendships, and interactions with our community.

Developing good relationships requires effective communication. Islam emphasises the importance of language and exhorts us to choose our words wisely. Any relationship will inevitably experience conflict, but how we handle it can make or break our bonds. Islam advises us to handle disputes with discernment, forbearance, and humility. In Islam, compassion and empathy are essential for creating wholesome relationships.

Engaging in Acts of Kindness and Charity (Sadaqah)

Acts of kindness and charity are powerful tools for strengthening both personal and communal bonds. These acts promote compassion, empathy, and a sense of shared responsibility, essential for nurturing strong relationships and a supportive community.

Promoting Compassion and Empathy

Engaging in charitable deeds, whether through financial contributions, volunteering time, or offering support to those in need, enhances one's sense of empathy and compassion. These acts of kindness not only help those who receive them but also foster a deeper sense of connection and understanding within the giver.

Charitable actions create opportunities to meaningfully engage with others, encouraging a culture of mutual respect and support. By participating in these acts, individuals and communities can collectively contribute to a more compassionate and empathetic society.

Strengthening Bonds of Brotherhood/Sisterhood (Ukhuwwah)

In faith communities, the concept of Ukhuwwah, or brotherhood/sisterhood, underscores the importance of mutual support and unity. Strengthening these bonds involves sharing joys and sorrows and actively participating in each other's lives through acts of kindness and support.

Building Ukhuwwah requires intentional efforts to understand and address the needs of others within the community. This might include organising support groups, participating in community service, or simply being present for those in need. By reinforcing these bonds, communities create a network of support that extends beyond individual relationships, fostering a strong, interconnected community.

Chapter Eleven

Lessons from Prophetic Examples

In times of adversity, finding a source of strength and guidance is essential. For Muslims, the life and experiences of Prophet Muhammad (PBUH) serve as a profound example of resilience and perseverance. Allah (SWT) sent the Prophet Muhammad (PBUH) to us as a mentor in this world of trials and tribulations, teaching us how to face hardships while maintaining hope.

The life of the Holy Prophet (PBUH) serves as a source of inspiration and motivation for us to pursue perfection. The Prophet (PBUH) indeed faced greater trials than any other prophet before him. The Prophet (PBUH) and his fellow believers underwent great hardships to offer a way of redemption to the generations who would follow them. They built the foundation for the quick spread of Islam and the transformation.

Many Muslims are well aware of the fundamentals of the Prophet's (PBUH) life, including his birth in Makkah, his journey to Medina, many of his wars, and the capture of Makkah. The Prophet (PBUH) endured an incredible amount of trauma, suffering, and anguish, as one would discover upon closely reading the Prophet's Seerah.

Intense verbal and physical abuse, humiliation in public, family deaths, and other things happened to him. People's sensitivity to hardship varies, as we know, depending on the psychological and physical costs. Since the Prophet (PBUH) had the purest and gentlest of personalities, the difficulty of establishing Islam as a religion greatly troubled him.

His life, filled with trials and tribulations, offers valuable lessons on navigating and overcoming challenges with unwavering faith and strength. By studying the stories of the Prophets and righteous individuals, we can glean insights into resilience and apply these lessons to our own lives, fostering both personal success and spiritual growth.

Learning from the Prophetic Model of Resilience

Prophet Muhammad (PBUH) is revered not just as a spiritual leader but as a paragon of resilience. His life is a testament to enduring faith and fortitude in the face of overwhelming challenges. From the early days of his prophethood, he encountered intense opposition and hardship. He (PBUH) faced ridicule, persecution, and the loss of loved ones, yet he remained steadfast and unyielding in his mission.

One of the most profound lessons from his life is his ability to maintain hope and optimism despite facing immense difficulties. The early years of Islam were marked by significant trials, including the boycott of his clan, the harsh treatment of early Muslims, and the loss of his beloved wife, Hazrat Khadijah (RA), and his uncle, Hazrat Abu Talib (RA). Yet, the Prophet's (PBUH) response to these adversities was not despair but a deepened sense of purpose and resilience. He sought solace in his faith and continued his mission with unwavering dedication.

Another critical aspect of the Prophet's (PBUH) resilience was his strategic approach to overcoming obstacles. His migration (Hijra) to Medina is a prime example of how he adapted to changing circumstances while remaining true to his principles. This strategic move not only ensured the survival of the early Muslim community but also paved the way for the establishment of a thriving and supportive society.

Prophet Muhammad's (PBUH) life also underscores the importance of community and support systems in overcoming challenges. The bonds he forged with his companions, the Ansar (helpers) and the Muhajirun (migrants), were instrumental in creating a strong, resilient community capable of facing adversity together. This collective resilience highlights the value of mutual support and solidarity in times of hardship.

Studying the Stories of the Prophets and Righteous Individuals

Beyond the life of Prophet Muhammad (PBUH), the stories of other prophets and righteous individuals provide rich lessons in resilience. For instance, the story of Prophet Ibrahim (Abraham) (PBUH) demonstrates extraordinary faith and perseverance. His willingness to sacrifice his son, as commanded by Allah (SWT), is a profound example of trusting in divine wisdom despite personal loss and sacrifice. The ultimate divine intervention that spared his son highlights the reward of unwavering faith and patience.

Similarly, the story of Prophet Yusuf (Joseph) (PBUH) is a powerful narrative of patience and eventual triumph. Betrayed by his brothers and sold into slavery, Prophet Yusuf (PBUH) faced numerous trials but remained steadfast in his faith. His eventual rise to a position of power in Egypt and his reunion with his family underscores the themes of patience, forgiveness, and divine justice.

The stories of these prophets illustrate how resilience is not merely about enduring hardships but also about maintaining faith and integrity throughout the journey. They teach us that challenges are part of a larger divine plan, and through perseverance, faith, and righteous conduct, we can overcome obstacles and achieve spiritual and personal growth.

Embracing Resilience for Success and Spiritual Growth

Applying the lessons of resilience from the Prophetic examples can have a profound impact on our lives. Embracing these strategies helps navigate life's daily challenges and fosters a deeper sense of inner peace and success.

Islamic strategies for resilience emphasise the importance of faith, patience, and reliance on Allah. By integrating these principles into our lives, we can approach difficulties with a sense of purpose and tranquillity. Faith-based resilience practices, such as regular prayer, supplication, and reflection, provide strength and guidance. These practices help us maintain a positive outlook and find hope even in the face of adversity.

Incorporating the lessons from the Prophetic model into our daily lives encourages us to face challenges with courage and optimism. It inspires us to build supportive communities, seek solace in faith, and approach difficulties with patience and perseverance. By doing so, we enhance our chances of achieving success and cultivate spiritual growth and inner peace.

The life of Prophet Muhammad (PBUH) and the stories of other Prophets offer timeless lessons in resilience. Their experiences remind us that challenges are an inherent part of life and that our response to them defines our path to success and spiritual fulfilment. By drawing inspiration from these prophetic examples and applying their teachings, we can navigate life's trials with grace, hope, and unwavering faith.

Chapter Twelve

Conclusion

I hope this book has offered a valuable roadmap for developing resilience through the enduring principles of Islam. Life is inevitably full of trials, but how we respond to them greatly influences our emotional and spiritual health.

The emphasis that true resilience goes beyond mere endurance; it involves transforming hardships into opportunities for personal growth and spiritual upliftment.

By comprehending the nature of life's challenges and the concept of divine decree (Qadr), you're encouraged to adopt a mindset that faces uncertainty with trust in Allah's wisdom. This trust, or Tawakkul, is the cornerstone of spiritual resilience, allowing you to approach even the most difficult trials with peace and purpose.

Through the consistent application of Sabr (patience), along with reliance on Salah (prayer) and Dua (supplication), you can find solace and strength during adversity.

The book also stresses the importance of maintaining emotional wellness and seeking knowledge as key aspects of resilience. By integrating Islamic teachings into everyday decisions, you can develop a balanced approach to life's challenges, ensuring your faith remains a source of comfort and guidance.

We've highlighted the significance of social support, kindness, and community engagement in reinforcing resilience, reminding you that you're alone in your struggles. Ultimately, this book encourages embracing resilience as a journey toward both worldly success and spiritual fulfilment, with faith as the guiding force.

Find Out More

Website: www.barakahinbusiness.com

Socials: @barakahinbusiness

If you enjoyed this book, kindly leave a review to help expand our reach so others may benefit also.

www.ingramcontent.com/pod-product-compliance
Lightning Source LLC
Chambersburg PA
CBHW052040150726
48002CB00002B/692